Post-IPO Wealth Strategies and Liquidity Management

How to Manage Stock Sales, Taxes, and Wealth After Going Public

By Joe Correa

Published by Live Stronger Faster

This book is for educational and informational purposes only. The author and publisher are not engaged in rendering legal, financial, or other professional advice. Readers should consult a qualified professional before making any financial decisions.

First Edition

Table of Contents

Introduction

Going public is often viewed as the ultimate finish line for entrepreneurs, startup founders, executives, and early investors. The ringing of the opening bell, media attention, surging stock prices, and sudden visibility can create the appearance that the financial journey is complete. Yet in reality, the IPO is not the end of the wealth creation process—it is the beginning of an entirely new and far more complex financial phase. Many individuals spend years focused on building a company strong enough to reach the public markets, but surprisingly few prepare themselves for what comes after the IPO. The transition from private ownership to public market liquidity changes everything. It changes how wealth is managed, taxed, protected, diversified, and ultimately preserved for future generations.

This book exists because post-IPO wealth management is one of the most misunderstood areas in business and finance. A founder may suddenly hold tens of millions—or even hundreds of millions—of dollars in publicly traded shares, yet still face enormous financial risks. Wealth that appears substantial on paper can disappear quickly due to poor liquidity planning, emotional stock sales, market crashes, tax inefficiencies, overconcentration, legal exposure, or lifestyle inflation.

History is filled with stories of founders, executives, and early employees who became wealthy during an IPO only to lose a significant portion of that wealth within a few years. In contrast, others used strategic liquidity management to create permanent, multi-generational wealth that lasted long after the initial public offering.

The difference between these two outcomes rarely comes down to luck alone. It comes down to preparation, education, emotional discipline, and strategic planning. Post-IPO wealth is not simply about owning stock. It is about understanding timing, taxation, diversification, risk management, estate planning, capital preservation, and long-term financial architecture. The individuals who successfully transition from "paper wealth" to enduring wealth understand that liquidity is both an opportunity and a responsibility. They recognize that wealth management after an IPO requires just as much sophistication as building the business itself.

One of the first realities founders encounter after going public is that liquidity does not happen instantly. Although a company may now trade publicly on the stock market, insider lockup periods often restrict executives and early investors from immediately selling shares. These lockups may last several months, during which stock prices can fluctuate dramatically. During this time, emotions become dangerous. A rapidly rising stock price can create overconfidence and encourage reckless financial decisions, while falling share prices can create fear, panic, and impulsive selling. Understanding the psychology of liquidity becomes just as important as understanding financial strategy.

Another major challenge emerges in the form of taxes. Many entrepreneurs spend years focused almost entirely on growing revenue, attracting investors, hiring teams, and scaling operations. Yet after an IPO, taxes suddenly become one of the most important factors affecting long-term wealth. Capital gains taxes, alternative minimum tax exposure, stock option taxation, restricted stock unit planning, state tax residency strategies, charitable giving structures, and estate transfer techniques all become critical areas of focus. Without proper planning, enormous portions of IPO-generated wealth can disappear unnecessarily through inefficient tax structures.

This is especially true for founders and executives who receive compensation through stock options or equity grants. A single exercise decision can create millions of dollars in tax liability. Selling too early can trigger unnecessary taxation, while holding too long may expose wealth to market volatility. Managing concentrated stock positions becomes one of the most difficult balancing acts in post-IPO finance. Many founders emotionally believe in their company so deeply that they refuse to diversify, even when their personal financial future depends almost entirely on one stock. Unfortunately, financial history repeatedly demonstrates the danger of overconcentration. Companies that once appeared unstoppable can decline unexpectedly due to economic cycles, competition, regulation, technological disruption, or management failures.

This book will help readers understand how sophisticated investors and founders navigate these risks. It will explore the frameworks used to protect wealth while maintaining exposure to long-term upside potential. Readers will learn how diversification strategies work, how liquidity schedules are planned, how family offices operate, and how high-net-worth individuals structure portfolios after major equity events. The goal is not simply to preserve money. The goal is to convert temporary financial success into sustainable, long-term financial freedom.

As companies transition into public market environments, founders also encounter an entirely new relationship with volatility. In private markets, valuation updates may occur infrequently, sometimes only during funding rounds. In public markets, however, company valuation changes every second the market is open. This creates emotional pressure unlike anything experienced during the private phase of business ownership. A founder's net worth may fluctuate by millions of dollars in a single trading day. News headlines, earnings reports, analyst opinions, interest rate changes, and broader market sentiment can suddenly impact personal wealth in dramatic ways.

This emotional volatility often leads to dangerous decision-making. Some founders become obsessed with short-term stock price movements and lose focus on long-term strategy. Others make aggressive investments during bull markets only to suffer heavy losses during downturns. Wealth preservation requires emotional maturity and disciplined systems. One of the core lessons throughout this book is that financial freedom is not achieved through emotional reactions—it is achieved through structured planning and long-term thinking.

The transition from entrepreneur to wealthy public shareholder also introduces lifestyle risks. Many individuals dramatically increase spending immediately after an IPO. Expensive homes, luxury cars, private travel, speculative investments, and social pressure can quickly inflate monthly obligations. While these expenses may seem manageable during strong stock performance, market downturns can create financial strain if liquidity planning was poor. True wealth is not defined by temporary spending power. True wealth is defined by financial resilience, flexibility, and the ability to sustain freedom regardless of market conditions. Another important concept explored throughout this book is the idea of "wealth identity." Many founders spend years identifying themselves entirely through their company. After liquidity events occur, they may struggle emotionally with purpose, direction, and financial identity. Some continue taking unnecessary risks because they feel uncomfortable transitioning from builder to steward. Others experience anxiety about preserving wealth they worked years to create. Post-IPO wealth management is therefore not just financial—it is psychological. Sustainable wealth requires a healthy relationship with money, purpose, and long-term vision.

Readers will also discover how some of the world's wealthiest entrepreneurs transformed IPO liquidity into diversified investment empires. Many founders use post-IPO capital to acquire real estate, private companies, venture investments, dividend-producing assets, and alternative investments. Others establish charitable foundations, donor-advised funds, or family offices designed to manage wealth across generations. Understanding these structures provides insight into how significant wealth evolves beyond a single company or liquidity event.

This book will explore practical post-IPO strategies including staged stock sales, tax-loss harvesting, charitable remainder trusts, opportunity zone investing, estate transfer planning, liquidity forecasting, portfolio allocation, insurance strategies, risk mitigation, and long-term capital preservation. It will also explain how wealth advisors, tax attorneys, estate planners, investment bankers, and family office professionals collaborate to protect large financial positions. Readers will gain a realistic understanding of what it actually takes to manage substantial wealth responsibly after going public.

Importantly, this book is not only for billion-dollar founders. The principles discussed here apply to anyone experiencing equity-based wealth creation. Early employees with stock options, startup executives, angel investors, private shareholders, and entrepreneurs preparing for acquisitions or liquidity events can all benefit from understanding how wealth behaves after major financial transitions. Financial success does not automatically create financial intelligence. Education remains essential regardless of net worth level.

Throughout this series, readers have learned how companies go public, how valuations are created, how capital markets function, and how founders generate wealth through equity ownership. This book builds on those foundations by focusing on the next critical phase: protecting, managing, and expanding wealth after liquidity becomes real. Going public creates opportunity, but preserving and multiplying wealth requires discipline, structure, and advanced financial thinking. The public markets have created some of the greatest fortunes in modern history. Yet they have also destroyed fortunes for those who failed to prepare for the realities of liquidity management. Wealth can disappear much faster than it was created when risk is ignored or emotional decisions dominate financial planning. This book aims to provide the frameworks, mindset, and strategic understanding necessary to avoid those outcomes.

By the end of this book, readers will understand that post-IPO wealth management is not about fear—it is about control. It is about creating systems that allow wealth to survive economic cycles, market volatility, taxation, legal risk, and generational transitions. It is about converting financial success into lasting security and freedom. Most importantly, it is about ensuring that the years spent building a company ultimately result in a life of stability, opportunity, flexibility, and meaningful impact.

The IPO may create wealth, but what happens afterward determines whether that wealth becomes temporary or permanent.

Chapter 1

Understanding Post-IPO Wealth Reality: From Paper Wealth to Real Financial Control

For many entrepreneurs, executives, and early investors, the moment a company goes public represents the realization of years—or even decades—of sacrifice, stress, risk-taking, and relentless persistence. The IPO often appears to outsiders as the grand finale of the entrepreneurial journey. Media headlines celebrate billion-dollar valuations, founders ring the opening bell at stock exchanges, employees celebrate stock options becoming valuable, and financial analysts discuss future growth projections. Yet behind the scenes, one of the most important transitions is only beginning. The shift from private ownership to public liquidity fundamentally changes how wealth is experienced, managed, protected, and preserved. Many founders discover that becoming wealthy on paper is entirely different from building lasting financial security in reality.

One of the biggest misconceptions surrounding IPOs is the belief that founders immediately gain unrestricted access to enormous amounts of cash. In reality, post-IPO wealth is usually highly concentrated in company stock, restricted by lockup agreements, vulnerable to market volatility, and heavily influenced by tax consequences. A founder may technically become worth hundreds of millions of dollars overnight while still lacking immediate liquid cash access. This creates a dangerous psychological disconnect between perceived wealth and actual financial flexibility. The public may view the founder as extremely wealthy, yet much of that wealth remains tied to stock price fluctuations and future market performance.

This concept is often referred to as "paper wealth." Paper wealth represents theoretical net worth based on the current market value of shares owned. While this wealth can be substantial, it is not fully realized until shares are strategically sold and converted into diversified assets or liquid capital. Many newly public founders fail to fully understand this distinction. They begin increasing spending immediately after the IPO, assuming future stock appreciation will continue indefinitely. Luxury homes, exotic cars, private travel, speculative investments, and expensive lifestyles often follow rapidly rising stock prices. Unfortunately, history repeatedly demonstrates that stock prices do not move upward forever. Economic downturns, market corrections, competitive pressures, regulatory changes, or disappointing earnings can erase billions in market value within months. The dot-com era provides one of the clearest examples of this phenomenon.

During the late 1990s technology boom, countless founders and employees believed their stock options guaranteed permanent wealth. Companies with little profit and minimal sustainable revenue reached enormous valuations. Employees borrowed money against stock holdings, purchased expensive homes, and dramatically increased spending. When the technology bubble collapsed, many individuals discovered that their paper wealth had vanished almost overnight. Some lost not only their future wealth but also their savings, homes, and financial stability because their lifestyles had expanded based on temporary stock valuations.

The lesson from these events is not that IPOs are dangerous. Rather, the lesson is that liquidity management requires discipline, patience, and strategic planning. Post-IPO wealth should be approached as a long-term process instead of a short-term celebration. Founders who successfully preserve and grow wealth understand that their first responsibility after an IPO is risk management. Before aggressively pursuing additional returns, they focus on stabilizing their financial foundation. This often means diversifying assets, reducing concentrated exposure, planning for taxes, and establishing systems to protect wealth during future market cycles.

One of the most important concepts newly public shareholders must understand is concentration risk. Many founders hold the majority of their net worth in a single company stock. Emotionally, this makes sense. Founders believe deeply in the businesses they created. They may feel loyal to employees, investors, and customers. They often assume the company will continue growing indefinitely because they personally understand the business better than outside investors. However, concentration creates enormous vulnerability. If a single stock represents 70%, 80%, or even 90% of personal net worth, one major decline can dramatically reduce overall financial security.

Financial history is filled with examples of dominant companies experiencing severe declines. Industries evolve, technologies change, consumer behavior shifts, and economic conditions fluctuate. Even the most respected companies face uncertainty. Diversification exists not because investors lack confidence, but because uncertainty is unavoidable. Wealth preservation depends on preparing for outcomes that cannot be predicted with certainty. Sophisticated investors understand that protecting wealth matters just as much as creating it.

Another major challenge after going public involves emotional decision-making. During the private startup phase, founders often operate with extreme optimism and risk tolerance. Those traits are necessary to build companies in uncertain environments. However, the mindset that helps create wealth is not always the same mindset needed to preserve wealth. After an IPO, emotional discipline becomes essential. Public markets fluctuate daily. Stock prices react to earnings reports, analyst expectations, interest rate changes, geopolitical events, and investor sentiment. A founder's net worth may rise or fall by millions of dollars within hours.

This constant visibility creates psychological pressure. Some founders obsessively monitor stock prices throughout the day, allowing short-term fluctuations to influence emotions and decisions. Others become overconfident during bull markets and underestimate risk exposure. Fear and greed become powerful forces after liquidity events. Learning how to separate emotions from financial planning becomes one of the most important post-IPO skills.

Taxation also becomes dramatically more important after an IPO. In many cases, individuals are unprepared for the complexity of stock-related taxes. Exercising stock options, selling shares, receiving restricted stock units, or relocating between states can create significant tax implications. Some founders discover that they owe millions in taxes even before fully liquidating stock positions. Without proper planning, taxes can consume a massive portion of wealth unnecessarily.

For example, incentive stock options may trigger alternative minimum tax exposure. Restricted stock units may create taxable income upon vesting. Large capital gains from stock sales can create federal and state tax liabilities exceeding expectations. High-income individuals may also face additional surtaxes or estate planning concerns. Understanding tax strategy becomes critical because preserving wealth often depends less on investment returns and more on efficient tax management.

Sophisticated post-IPO planning frequently begins years before shares are sold. Wealthy founders often work closely with tax attorneys, estate planners, investment advisors, and family office professionals to structure liquidity strategies in advance. Some establish charitable trusts, donor-advised funds, or gifting programs before stock appreciation accelerates further. Others relocate to tax-friendly states before liquidity events occur. Timing becomes incredibly important because once taxable events occur, many planning opportunities disappear permanently.

Another overlooked aspect of post-IPO wealth management is liquidity timing. Even after lockup periods expire, selling large blocks of stock requires careful planning. Sudden insider selling may negatively impact market perception and stock prices. Securities regulations may limit trading windows for executives. Some founders use Rule 10b5-1 trading plans, which establish predetermined selling schedules designed to reduce emotional decision-making and regulatory concerns. These plans help executives gradually diversify holdings while maintaining compliance with insider trading regulations.

The transition from entrepreneur to wealthy public shareholder also changes how personal relationships operate. Friends, family members, investors, and business contacts may suddenly view the founder differently after an IPO. Requests for investments, loans, business opportunities, and financial support often increase significantly. Some individuals struggle with guilt or pressure related to wealth visibility. Others experience isolation because relationships become influenced by financial status. Maintaining healthy boundaries and surrounding oneself with trustworthy advisors becomes increasingly important.

Many founders also underestimate the importance of personal identity after liquidity events. During the startup phase, life revolves around building the company. Long hours, intense stress, constant problem-solving, and mission-driven focus dominate daily existence. After an IPO, however, some founders feel emotionally disoriented. Financial success may not provide the fulfillment they expected. Without a clear sense of purpose beyond the company, some individuals become restless, anxious, or depressed despite substantial wealth. This psychological transition explains why many successful entrepreneurs eventually pursue philanthropy, mentorship, investing, or new ventures. Long-term fulfillment usually requires purpose beyond financial accumulation alone. Wealth provides options, flexibility, and security, but meaningful direction still matters deeply. Post-IPO planning should therefore include not only financial strategy but also lifestyle and personal vision planning.

One of the smartest moves many newly wealthy founders make is slowing down major decisions during the first year after an IPO. Sudden wealth can create emotional excitement that leads to impulsive behavior. Large purchases, risky investments, or dramatic lifestyle changes often feel justified after years of sacrifice. Yet the most financially successful individuals frequently adopt the opposite approach. They spend time building advisory teams, studying wealth management principles, and creating long-term strategies before making major financial commitments.

This period of stabilization allows founders to transition gradually from growth-focused entrepreneurs into disciplined capital allocators. Instead of relying solely on aggressive business instincts, they begin thinking in terms of portfolio management, risk-adjusted returns, tax efficiency, and multi-generational wealth planning. The mindset shift is substantial. Building wealth and preserving wealth are related skills, but they are not identical.

Another critical reality of post-IPO life is understanding that markets move in cycles. Bull markets create optimism, rising valuations, and easy access to capital. Bear markets create fear, contraction, and uncertainty. Wealthy individuals who survive across multiple decades recognize the importance of preparing for both environments. They maintain liquidity reserves, diversify income streams, reduce unnecessary leverage, and avoid becoming dependent on permanently rising stock prices.

Many founders eventually realize that the ultimate goal is not maximizing short-term net worth. The ultimate goal is achieving durable freedom. Durable freedom means having enough diversified assets, cash flow, and financial stability to live independently of market fluctuations or business performance. This often requires shifting from a concentrated growth mindset toward a balanced wealth preservation mindset.

The public markets have created extraordinary wealth for countless entrepreneurs and investors. Yet they have also exposed many individuals to risks they never previously encountered. Going public creates visibility, liquidity potential, and financial opportunity, but it also introduces volatility, taxation, emotional pressure, and complexity. The founders who navigate this transition successfully are usually those who approach post-IPO wealth management with humility, discipline, patience, and long-term thinking.

The journey from paper wealth to real financial control does not happen automatically. It requires intentional planning, education, emotional maturity, and strategic execution. Understanding this reality is the first step toward transforming temporary market success into lasting financial security. The IPO may create the opportunity for wealth, but the decisions made afterward determine whether that wealth becomes permanent, sustainable, and meaningful for generations to come.

The Founder Who Almost Lost Everything After Going Public

Daniel Rivera sat quietly in the backseat of a black SUV as it rolled through lower Manhattan before sunrise. Outside the tinted windows, television crews were already gathering near the stock exchange. Reporters adjusted cameras while employees from his company waved signs and celebrated on the sidewalk. Today was the day everyone had talked about for years. His company, Nexora Systems, was officially going public.

Only ten years earlier, Daniel had been coding software alone in a cramped apartment with unpaid bills stacked on the kitchen table. He remembered eating instant noodles for dinner while trying to convince investors to believe in his vision. Friends thought he was reckless for quitting a stable engineering job. His parents worried constantly about his future. There were months when payroll barely cleared. Some early employees worked for reduced salaries because they believed in the mission. Those years felt endless.

Now investment bankers estimated Daniel's shares were worth over $480 million at the IPO price.

The driver glanced in the mirror. "Big day, huh?"

Daniel smiled weakly. "I guess so."

But deep inside, he felt strangely disconnected from the celebration. Everyone around him acted as though he had already won. Yet he knew most of his wealth existed only on screens and spreadsheets. He could not sell shares immediately because of insider lockup agreements. The money was technically his, but not fully accessible. Even so, the pressure had already begun.

His phone buzzed constantly.

Friends he had not spoken to in years suddenly wanted to reconnect. Venture capital firms pitched investment opportunities. Luxury real estate agents sent listings for waterfront mansions. Family members hinted at financial support for business ideas. Private banks invited him to exclusive wealth management dinners. The attention felt overwhelming.

When Nexora's stock opened 40% above the IPO price that morning, the financial media exploded with excitement. Headlines called Daniel "the next great tech billionaire." Analysts predicted the stock would double again within a year. Employees celebrated wildly inside the company headquarters.

That night, Daniel attended an exclusive rooftop party overlooking the city skyline. Investors toasted champagne glasses while music echoed across the terrace.

"You're set for life," one executive told him. "Now you enjoy it."

At first, Daniel tried to stay grounded. But over the following months, something slowly changed. The stock continued climbing aggressively. Financial news channels praised Nexora almost daily. His paper net worth crossed $700 million.

The rising stock price made everything feel possible.

Daniel purchased a massive modern mansion in Miami. Then came a private jet membership. He invested millions into several speculative startups recommended by wealthy friends. He bought luxury vehicles he barely drove. His monthly spending quietly exploded.

At the same time, he refused to sell meaningful amounts of Nexora stock.

"I built this company," he told advisors repeatedly. "Why would I sell something that's still growing?"

His financial advisor, Karen Mitchell, warned him carefully during one meeting.

"You're too concentrated," she explained. "Almost all your net worth depends on one stock. You should gradually diversify."

Daniel shook his head confidently. "You don't understand Nexora like I do. We're just getting started."

Karen remained calm. "Every founder says that before market cycles change."

But Daniel ignored the advice.

Over the next year, economic conditions shifted. Interest rates rose sharply. Technology valuations began falling across the market. Investors suddenly became more cautious. Growth stocks that once soared started collapsing.

At first, Daniel stayed optimistic. "It's temporary," he told employees. Then Nexora missed quarterly earnings expectations by a small margin.

The stock dropped 18% in a single day.

Daniel stared silently at his computer screen that night. Tens of millions of dollars disappeared from his paper net worth within hours. Yet he still refused to sell.

Months later, a larger competitor announced a competing product line that threatened Nexora's market share. Analysts downgraded the stock aggressively.

Another massive decline followed.

The pressure intensified quickly. Daniel's expensive lifestyle suddenly felt dangerous. Some of his speculative startup investments were already failing. Property values softened. Meanwhile, tax obligations from earlier stock exercises remained enormous.

For the first time in years, Daniel struggled to sleep.

He realized something terrifying: despite being "worth" hundreds of millions on paper only a year earlier, much of his actual wealth remained vulnerable.

One evening he sat alone in his dark office while reviewing financial reports. Karen entered quietly. "You finally ready to talk?" she asked gently.

Daniel sighed heavily. "I thought holding everything showed confidence."

Karen nodded. "Confidence is important. But wealth preservation requires balance."

Over the next several months, Daniel completely changed his approach to money.

He established a structured diversification plan. Instead of emotional reactions, he used scheduled selling programs. He reduced unnecessary spending dramatically. He built a diversified portfolio including bonds, dividend investments, private equity, real estate, and cash reserves. He worked with tax professionals to create long-term estate planning structures. He stopped obsessively checking Nexora's stock price every hour.

Most importantly, he changed psychologically.

For years Daniel believed wealth meant having the highest possible net worth. Eventually he realized real wealth meant stability, flexibility, and peace of mind.

Five years later, Nexora remained a successful public company, though its stock price never again reached the euphoric highs of the IPO era. Many early employees who ignored diversification had lost most of their paper fortunes during market declines.

Daniel, however, survived the cycle.

He no longer chased headlines or temporary valuations. His diversified assets generated sustainable income regardless of stock market conditions. He funded educational programs for young entrepreneurs. He mentored startup founders preparing for their own liquidity events. He spent more time with family and regained a sense of balance that had disappeared during the frenzy of rapid wealth.

During an interview years later, a journalist asked him a simple question.

"What was the biggest lesson after going public?"

Daniel paused thoughtfully before answering.

"An IPO can make you rich on paper," he said quietly. "But real wealth begins the moment you learn how not to lose it."

Chapter 2

Managing Concentrated Stock Positions and Diversification After an IPO

One of the greatest financial challenges faced by founders, executives, and early employees after a company goes public is managing concentrated stock exposure. During the startup phase, concentration is often unavoidable. Founders build businesses by dedicating nearly all of their energy, time, and financial risk toward a single company. Equity ownership becomes the reward for years of uncertainty and sacrifice. By the time the company reaches an IPO, that ownership may represent the overwhelming majority of the founder's personal net worth. While this concentration helped create wealth, it can become one of the greatest threats to preserving wealth after liquidity arrives.

Concentrated stock positions create a unique financial paradox. The same asset that generated extraordinary financial success can also become the primary source of future financial vulnerability. Many newly wealthy founders emotionally struggle with this reality because their company stock represents more than just money. It symbolizes identity, belief, loyalty, achievement, and personal sacrifice. Selling shares may feel emotionally uncomfortable, almost as if they are betraying the company or signaling a lack of confidence in the future. Yet diversification is not about abandoning belief in a business. Diversification is about protecting financial stability from the unpredictable nature of markets and economic cycles.

Public market history repeatedly demonstrates that even dominant companies can experience severe declines. Industries change rapidly. Consumer behavior evolves. Economic downturns impact valuations. New technologies disrupt existing business models. Regulatory environments shift unexpectedly. Competitive advantages weaken over time. Some companies recover from market declines, while others never return to previous highs. Concentration risk becomes dangerous because it exposes personal wealth to the fate of a single organization, regardless of how strong that company may appear today.

Many founders mistakenly believe their deep understanding of the business protects them from concentration risk. While insider knowledge may provide confidence in operational performance, it does not eliminate external risks. Broader market conditions, investor sentiment, interest rate changes, geopolitical instability, legal issues, or macroeconomic recessions can dramatically impact stock prices regardless of company fundamentals. Public markets often move based on fear and emotion as much as logic. Even exceptional businesses experience volatility that can threaten highly concentrated personal balance sheets.

The emotional attachment founders have toward their companies often creates psychological resistance to diversification. Some believe that selling shares communicates weakness to investors or employees. Others fear missing future upside if the stock continues climbing. There is also a common mindset among entrepreneurs that they succeeded by taking concentrated risks in the past, so they should continue doing so. However, the mindset required to create wealth is not always the same mindset needed to preserve wealth. Entrepreneurs build wealth through concentration and aggressive conviction. Wealth preservation, however, often requires measured risk reduction and strategic balance.

One of the biggest mistakes post-IPO shareholders make is waiting too long to diversify. During strong bull markets, rising stock prices reinforce emotional attachment and overconfidence. As valuations increase, founders become even more reluctant to sell because future gains appear limitless. Yet market cycles eventually change. When declines begin, many individuals hesitate to sell because they hope prices will recover quickly. This emotional paralysis can trap shareholders in devastating downward cycles. The inability to separate emotional belief from rational financial planning destroys significant wealth every market cycle.

Diversification serves one primary purpose: survival. The goal is not necessarily to maximize the highest possible return. The goal is to ensure long-term financial independence regardless of what happens to one individual company. Sophisticated investors understand that protecting downside risk is just as important as participating in upside opportunity. Financial freedom becomes more sustainable when wealth is distributed across multiple asset classes, industries, and income streams rather than relying entirely on one stock.

One common diversification strategy involves gradual stock liquidation over time. Instead of attempting to predict perfect market tops or bottoms, many founders implement systematic selling schedules. This approach reduces emotional decision-making and lowers the pressure associated with market timing. Selling portions of shares consistently over months or years allows shareholders to reduce concentration while still maintaining meaningful ownership exposure. Gradual diversification also helps minimize sudden tax consequences and avoids sending negative signals to the market through massive insider sales.

Rule 10b5-1 trading plans have become particularly important tools for executives managing public company stock. These plans establish predetermined schedules for future stock sales, helping executives avoid accusations of insider trading while reducing emotional reactions to short-term market fluctuations. Because trades are planned in advance, the process becomes more disciplined and systematic. Many successful founders use these structures to gradually convert concentrated stock positions into diversified portfolios over time.

Diversification after an IPO often extends far beyond simply selling shares and holding cash. Wealthy founders typically allocate capital into multiple categories designed to balance growth, stability, income generation, and inflation protection. Public equities, private equity investments, real estate, bonds, venture capital, dividend-producing assets, infrastructure investments, and alternative assets may all play roles within diversified wealth strategies. Each asset class behaves differently during economic cycles, reducing the likelihood that all wealth sources decline simultaneously.

Real estate frequently becomes a major diversification target for newly public entrepreneurs. Income-producing real estate offers several advantages, including cash flow generation, inflation protection, leverage opportunities, and long-term appreciation potential. Multifamily housing, industrial real estate, self-storage facilities, commercial properties, and vacation rental investments often attract founders seeking stable assets outside the stock market. Real estate also provides psychological comfort because it represents tangible ownership rather than purely digital market valuations.

Some founders diversify into private investments and venture capital opportunities. Having built successful companies themselves, they may enjoy mentoring younger entrepreneurs while gaining exposure to emerging industries. However, private investing introduces additional risk and illiquidity. Without discipline, founders can become overexposed to speculative startup investments that lack stable cash flow or predictable valuations. Diversification works best when balanced across both growth-oriented and defensive assets.

Fixed-income investments also play an important role in wealth preservation. While entrepreneurs often dislike lower-return investments emotionally, bonds and fixed-income securities provide stability during volatile equity markets. High-quality fixed-income assets can preserve purchasing power, generate predictable income, and create liquidity reserves for future opportunities. Wealth preservation is not always exciting, but stability becomes increasingly valuable after achieving significant financial success. Cash reserves are another overlooked component of post-IPO diversification. During strong markets, holding large cash positions may appear inefficient because cash generates relatively low returns. Yet liquidity provides flexibility during economic uncertainty. Cash reserves allow investors to avoid forced selling during downturns while creating the ability to acquire attractive assets when valuations decline. Many successful investors build wealth not merely by participating in bull markets, but by having liquidity available during periods of panic and market dislocation.

Another critical aspect of diversification involves geographic and currency exposure. Some founders maintain nearly all assets within a single country or economic system. However, global diversification can reduce exposure to domestic economic weakness, political instability, or currency devaluation. International investments, foreign real estate holdings, and global business opportunities may strengthen long-term portfolio resilience. Wealth preservation increasingly requires understanding global economic interconnectedness.

Tax planning also influences diversification strategy. Selling large stock positions creates taxable events, and poorly timed liquidation can significantly reduce after-tax wealth. Sophisticated investors frequently coordinate diversification with tax-loss harvesting, charitable giving structures, trusts, installment sales, donor-advised funds, and state residency planning. Tax efficiency becomes one of the largest determinants of long-term wealth retention after liquidity events occur.

Estate planning intersects closely with diversification as well. Many founders initially focus entirely on wealth creation but later recognize the importance of protecting assets for future generations. Trust structures, gifting strategies, life insurance planning, and family partnerships may all help preserve wealth across decades while reducing future estate tax exposure. Diversification therefore becomes part of a larger wealth architecture rather than simply an investment decision.

Importantly, diversification does not mean abandoning entrepreneurial thinking. Some founders fear that diversification represents "playing it safe" or losing ambition. In reality, diversification can create greater freedom to pursue meaningful opportunities without risking total financial collapse. When personal financial security no longer depends entirely on one stock price, founders often think more clearly, take more strategic risks, and avoid emotionally driven financial behavior.

Another major benefit of diversification is psychological stability. Concentrated stock ownership creates constant emotional dependence on daily market fluctuations. Net worth volatility can produce stress, anxiety, overconfidence, or fear. Diversified portfolios reduce this emotional intensity by smoothing overall financial performance. Mental clarity improves when personal security is not tied exclusively to one earnings report or stock movement.

Diversification also allows wealth to evolve beyond a single company identity. Many founders initially define themselves entirely through their businesses. Over time, however, true financial maturity involves separating personal identity from any one asset or company. Wealth becomes a tool for creating flexibility, opportunities, security, impact, and freedom rather than merely representing ownership concentration.

The most financially successful founders often share one important characteristic: they survive multiple economic cycles. Longevity matters more than temporary valuation peaks. Many individuals become wealthy during bull markets, but far fewer preserve and grow wealth across decades. Diversification improves survival probability by reducing exposure to catastrophic outcomes. Wealth that survives downturns gains the opportunity to compound over long periods of time.

Post-IPO diversification ultimately requires humility. No company remains invincible forever. No founder can perfectly predict future market conditions. No industry is immune to disruption. The purpose of diversification is not pessimism—it is preparation. It acknowledges uncertainty while building systems designed to withstand it.

Founders who successfully manage concentrated stock positions understand that financial freedom depends not only on creating wealth but also on protecting it. The IPO may create opportunity, but diversification transforms opportunity into durability. Sustainable wealth is rarely built on emotional attachment alone. It is built through balance, discipline, strategic planning, and the willingness to evolve from entrepreneur into long-term steward of capital.

The Billion-Dollar Stock That Nearly Destroyed Ethan Cole

When Ethan Cole founded Luminary AI from a small coworking office in Austin, he never imagined his company would one day dominate headlines across global financial media. Back then, he was simply obsessed with solving a problem. Artificial intelligence tools were becoming more powerful, but businesses struggled to integrate them efficiently into daily operations. Ethan believed his software could simplify enterprise automation for companies around the world.

For seven years, he worked nonstop.

There were stretches when he slept on office couches, missed family gatherings, and lived almost entirely on caffeine and adrenaline. Investors rejected him repeatedly during the early stages. Several competitors with larger funding nearly pushed Luminary AI out of business. Yet Ethan remained relentless. Slowly, the company gained traction. Revenue exploded. Enterprise clients signed long-term contracts. Venture capital poured in.

By the time Luminary AI filed for its IPO, the company was valued at nearly $12 billion.

On the morning of the public offering, Ethan stood on the balcony overlooking the trading floor while cameras flashed around him. Financial journalists described him as a visionary founder. Analysts predicted Luminary AI would become one of the largest technology companies of the decade.

When trading opened, the stock surged nearly 70%.

Ethan's ownership stake was suddenly worth over $1.4 billion.

The number felt unreal.

His phone became impossible to manage. Wealth managers, private bankers, celebrities, startup founders, and investment firms all wanted access to him. Friends treated him differently. Even strangers stared at him differently during public appearances. But Ethan barely noticed the emotional shift happening inside himself. The rising stock price became addictive.

Every morning he checked Luminary AI's valuation before getting out of bed. Every financial news segment discussing the company triggered emotional highs or lows. As the stock climbed higher month after month, Ethan became convinced the momentum would continue indefinitely.

His longtime financial advisor, Rebecca Lin, scheduled several meetings to discuss diversification.

"You're dangerously concentrated," she warned carefully. "Almost everything you own depends on Luminary's stock."

Ethan leaned back confidently. "Because Luminary is changing the world."

Rebecca nodded. "That may be true. But markets don't care about confidence forever."

He dismissed the concern.

"I built this company from nothing," he said. "Selling now would be insane."

Instead of diversifying, Ethan doubled down psychologically. He borrowed against portions of his stock holdings to purchase luxury real estate in Miami, Aspen, and Malibu. He invested aggressively into speculative startups launched by other tech founders. He upgraded his lifestyle rapidly.

At first, everything seemed brilliant.

Luminary AI's stock continued climbing. Ethan's net worth crossed $2 billion on paper. Media outlets called him one of the richest self-made entrepreneurs in America.

Then the market changed.

Interest rates rose sharply across the economy. Technology stocks began collapsing as investors shifted toward safer assets. Companies once praised for rapid growth suddenly faced harsh scrutiny over profitability.

Luminary AI initially resisted the decline.

Then one quarterly earnings report changed everything.

Growth slowed slightly below analyst expectations.

The stock dropped 22% in one day.

Ethan remained calm publicly, but privately he panicked. Tens of millions of dollars disappeared almost instantly.

"It's temporary," he told himself repeatedly.

But the decline continued. Competitors entered the market aggressively. Enterprise clients reduced spending during the economic slowdown. Analysts downgraded the company. Investors became fearful.

Within nine months, Luminary AI's stock had fallen nearly 68% from its peak.

Ethan's paper fortune collapsed.

Suddenly, the loans tied to his stock positions created enormous pressure. Some lenders demanded additional collateral. Startup investments he had funded during the boom were failing rapidly. Expensive real estate holdings became difficult to manage. Tax obligations from earlier stock transactions remained enormous despite the market decline.

For the first time since founding the company, Ethan felt trapped.

One evening he sat alone in his Miami mansion staring at the ocean through massive glass windows. The house felt strangely empty despite its beauty.

Rebecca arrived for an emergency meeting.

"You need to stop thinking like a founder for a moment," she told him calmly.

Ethan looked exhausted. "What does that even mean?" "It means you already won," she said quietly. "But you never protected the victory."

Those words stayed with him.

Over the following year, Ethan completely rebuilt his financial life.

He sold portions of remaining stock methodically through structured plans. He reduced unnecessary leverage. He diversified into income-producing real estate, fixed-income investments, dividend portfolios, and private businesses with stable cash flow. He established trusts and long-term estate planning systems. Most importantly, he stopped emotionally tying his self-worth to Luminary AI's stock price.

The transition was painful at first.

For years he believed holding concentrated stock represented loyalty and conviction. Eventually he realized diversification was not betrayal—it was survival.

Five years later, Luminary AI remained a respected public company, though its valuation never returned to peak bubble levels. Many executives who refused to diversify lost the majority of their fortunes during the collapse.

Ethan, however, survived. His diversified portfolio generated stable income regardless of technology market volatility. He no longer obsessed over daily stock movements. He spent more time mentoring founders about liquidity management than discussing valuations.

During a private conference for entrepreneurs, a young founder once asked him a question.

"If you could change one thing after your IPO, what would it be?"

Ethan smiled thoughtfully before answering.

"I thought concentration made me powerful," he said. "What I learned is that diversification gave me freedom."

Chapter 3

Tax Strategies for Founders, Executives, and Early Shareholders After an IPO

One of the most important and least understood aspects of post-IPO wealth management is taxation. While founders and executives often spend years focusing intensely on product development, revenue growth, fundraising, hiring, and scaling operations, many enter the public markets with surprisingly limited understanding of how taxes will affect their newly created wealth. This lack of preparation can become extraordinarily expensive. A single poorly timed stock sale, option exercise, or liquidity event can trigger millions of dollars in avoidable tax liability. For this reason, sophisticated tax planning is not optional after an IPO—it becomes one of the most critical components of preserving long-term wealth.

Taxes influence nearly every major financial decision after a company goes public. The timing of stock sales, the structure of compensation, residency decisions, estate planning, charitable giving, trust structures, and portfolio diversification strategies all intersect with tax consequences. Wealthy individuals who ignore tax efficiency often lose substantial portions of their fortunes unnecessarily. In contrast, those who proactively build tax strategies before liquidity events occur are frequently able to preserve significantly more wealth across decades and generations.

One of the first realities newly public shareholders must understand is that stock-based wealth is taxed differently depending on the type of equity involved. Founders, executives, and employees may hold common shares, incentive stock options, non-qualified stock options, restricted stock units, founder shares, or early exercise shares. Each structure carries different tax rules and timing implications. Understanding these differences becomes essential because tax obligations may arise long before shareholders fully convert stock into cash.

Incentive stock options, commonly referred to as ISOs, are particularly important for startup employees and executives. ISOs can provide favorable long-term capital gains treatment if handled properly, but they also create significant complexity through the alternative minimum tax system. Many individuals exercise options expecting future appreciation, only to discover they owe large tax bills even if the stock price later declines. This creates one of the most dangerous tax traps in startup equity compensation.

For example, an employee may exercise shares while the stock price is high, triggering alternative minimum tax liability based on the spread between exercise price and fair market value. If the stock subsequently falls before shares are sold, the individual may still owe taxes on gains that no longer exist economically. During previous technology market collapses, some employees faced devastating financial outcomes because they exercised options near valuation peaks and became trapped by tax obligations after stock prices collapsed.

Restricted stock units, or RSUs, create a different type of challenge. RSUs are typically taxed as ordinary income when they vest. This means executives may suddenly recognize large amounts of taxable income even if they do not immediately sell the shares. Because ordinary income tax rates are generally higher than long-term capital gains rates, strategic planning becomes essential. Some executives immediately sell portions of vested shares to cover taxes, while others coordinate broader diversification strategies alongside vesting schedules.

Founders holding common stock generally focus more heavily on capital gains taxation. Long-term capital gains rates are often substantially lower than ordinary income tax rates, creating strong incentives to hold shares for longer periods before selling. However, tax optimization cannot be viewed in isolation. Waiting too long to sell may expose wealth to excessive market risk. The challenge becomes balancing tax efficiency with diversification and risk management goals. This balancing act represents one of the most important post-IPO financial decisions. Many founders become so focused on minimizing taxes that they ignore concentration risk entirely. They hold enormous stock positions hoping to qualify for favorable long-term tax treatment while remaining dangerously exposed to market volatility. Others panic during downturns and sell too quickly, triggering unnecessary short-term tax exposure. Sophisticated wealth management requires integrating tax strategy with broader portfolio and liquidity planning.

State taxation also becomes critically important after an IPO. Many wealthy individuals underestimate how dramatically state residency impacts after-tax wealth. States such as California and New York impose high state income tax rates, while states like Florida and Texas do not impose state income taxes on individuals. For founders expecting large liquidity events, residency planning can potentially save millions or even tens of millions of dollars over time.

However, residency planning requires careful execution. States aggressively audit wealthy individuals attempting to establish residency elsewhere before liquidity events. Simply purchasing property in another state is usually insufficient. Residency determination may involve evaluating physical presence, driver's licenses, voter registration, business activities, family location, social connections, and numerous other factors. Poorly structured residency planning can result in lengthy legal disputes and unexpected tax exposure.

Another major tax consideration after an IPO involves charitable giving strategies. Many wealthy founders discover that philanthropy can serve both personal and financial purposes. Donating appreciated stock directly to qualified charitable organizations often allows individuals to avoid capital gains taxes while receiving charitable deductions. This creates an opportunity to support meaningful causes while improving tax efficiency simultaneously.

Donor-advised funds have become especially popular among entrepreneurs after liquidity events. These structures allow individuals to contribute appreciated stock, receive immediate tax deductions, and distribute charitable donations gradually over time. Charitable remainder trusts, private foundations, and family philanthropic vehicles also provide advanced planning opportunities for individuals seeking long-term wealth transfer and social impact strategies.

Estate planning becomes increasingly important once large equity positions become valuable. Many founders delay estate planning during the startup phase because company valuations remain uncertain. After an IPO, however, rapidly appreciating assets can create substantial future estate tax exposure. Without planning, significant portions of wealth may eventually transfer to governments rather than family members or charitable initiatives.

Trust structures often play a central role in post-IPO estate planning. Grantor retained annuity trusts, intentionally defective grantor trusts, dynasty trusts, and family limited partnerships may all help reduce taxable estates while preserving family wealth across generations. Some founders transfer shares into trusts before valuation increases accelerate further, maximizing long-term tax efficiency. Timing matters tremendously because planning opportunities often diminish once public market appreciation occurs.

Another advanced strategy involves qualified small business stock exemptions under Section 1202 of the Internal Revenue Code. Under certain conditions, founders and early investors may exclude significant portions of capital gains from federal taxation if shares meet specific holding period and qualification requirements. While these rules are highly technical, the potential tax savings can be enormous. Proper structuring during the private company phase can create substantial future benefits after an IPO or acquisition.

Tax-loss harvesting also becomes valuable for wealthy public shareholders. This strategy involves intentionally realizing investment losses to offset taxable gains elsewhere in a portfolio. During volatile markets, disciplined tax-loss harvesting can significantly improve after-tax investment returns over time. Sophisticated investors view taxes as part of the overall investment equation rather than treating them separately.

International taxation may also affect founders with global business operations, foreign investments, or international residency considerations. Cross-border tax planning becomes highly complex because multiple jurisdictions may claim taxing authority over income, capital gains, or assets. International entrepreneurs often require coordinated legal and accounting guidance to navigate treaties, foreign reporting requirements, and multinational tax structures effectively.

One of the most overlooked aspects of tax strategy is psychological behavior. Taxes often trigger emotional reactions that distort financial decision-making. Some individuals become so tax-averse that they refuse to diversify concentrated positions even when financial risk becomes dangerous. Others engage in aggressive tax schemes that create legal exposure and regulatory problems. Effective tax planning requires rational long-term thinking rather than emotional obsession with minimizing every possible tax dollar. The wealthiest individuals often focus not merely on avoiding taxes, but on maximizing after-tax outcomes over long periods of time. Sometimes paying taxes strategically creates better overall financial results than excessively delaying liquidity. Financial flexibility, diversification, peace of mind, and risk reduction all hold value beyond simple tax calculations. Wealth management should always evaluate the broader picture rather than focusing narrowly on short-term tax avoidance.

Family offices and sophisticated wealth management teams frequently integrate tax planning into every major financial decision. Investment structures, insurance strategies, real estate ownership, trust administration, philanthropic planning, and business succession all operate within coordinated tax frameworks. As wealth increases, tax efficiency becomes increasingly important because even small percentage improvements can translate into massive dollar savings over time.

Another important principle is recognizing that tax laws evolve constantly. Governments change policies, adjust rates, modify exemptions, and introduce new regulations regularly. Strategies that work effectively today may become less attractive in future years. Long-term wealth preservation therefore requires adaptability and ongoing professional guidance rather than one-time planning alone. Many founders initially resist spending money on elite tax advisors, attorneys, and wealth planners because they built businesses by operating leanly and controlling expenses aggressively. However, sophisticated advisory teams often save clients far more money than they cost. High-level planning becomes especially valuable when managing nine-figure or billion-dollar liquidity events where mistakes carry enormous consequences.

Importantly, tax planning should begin long before shares are sold. The best strategies are often proactive rather than reactive. Waiting until after liquidity events occur may eliminate valuable planning opportunities permanently. Founders preparing for IPOs benefit tremendously from assembling experienced legal, accounting, and financial teams early in the process.

Ultimately, taxes represent one of the largest forces influencing long-term wealth preservation after an IPO. Creating wealth through equity ownership is only the first step. Protecting that wealth requires understanding how taxation interacts with investment decisions, liquidity timing, diversification strategies, estate structures, and charitable planning. Founders who ignore tax strategy often discover too late that avoidable liabilities dramatically reduced their financial freedom.

The goal of sophisticated tax planning is not merely to avoid taxes. The goal is to create sustainable financial flexibility while preserving wealth across decades and generations. Effective planning transforms temporary liquidity into lasting opportunity. It allows founders, executives, and investors to retain greater control over the wealth they worked years to build. In the post-IPO world, understanding taxation becomes just as important as understanding business growth itself.

The Tax Bill That Changed Olivia Grant's Life

Olivia Grant still remembered the exact moment her life changed forever.

She was sitting inside a crowded conference room at Apex Quantum Technologies while employees watched the company's IPO launch live on giant television screens. Cheers erupted as the stock surged nearly 60% above its offering price within the first hour of trading. Champagne bottles popped. Executives hugged one another emotionally.

Olivia sat quietly near the back of the room staring at her phone.

According to the latest valuation update, her equity stake was now worth over $94 million.

Ten years earlier, she had joined Apex Quantum as employee number fourteen. Back then the company operated from a converted warehouse with unreliable air conditioning and folding tables instead of proper desks. Salaries were low. The future was uncertain. Friends told her she was making a terrible career decision by leaving a stable corporate finance position.

But Olivia believed in the company's vision.

For years she worked exhausting hours helping Apex scale globally. She accepted lower compensation in exchange for stock options because she believed long-term ownership mattered more than immediate salary. That decision ultimately changed her financial future.

After the IPO, however, Olivia quickly discovered that wealth created entirely new problems she never expected.

At first, everything felt exciting. Financial media called Apex one of the hottest technology companies in the world. The stock continued climbing aggressively during the months following the IPO. Olivia's net worth crossed $120 million on paper.

Friends congratulated her constantly.

“You never have to worry about money again,” one former coworker told her.

But beneath the excitement, Olivia began feeling uneasy. Most of her wealth remained tied to Apex stock. She could not freely sell large amounts because of lockup restrictions and insider trading rules. At the same time, tax complexity was becoming overwhelming.

One afternoon she met with her longtime accountant, Mark Feldman.

He reviewed several documents silently before looking up seriously.

“You exercised a significant amount of incentive stock options last year,” he explained.

Olivia nodded. “Everyone said it was smart because the stock would keep climbing.”

Mark sighed carefully. “The problem is the alternative minimum tax.”

Olivia frowned. “What does that mean?”

"It means you may owe taxes based on gains you haven't fully realized yet."

Her stomach tightened.

"How much?"

Mark paused.

"Approximately $11.8 million." The room suddenly felt cold.

Olivia stared at him in disbelief. "That can't be right."

Mark slid several spreadsheets across the table.

"The taxes were triggered when you exercised the options. The valuation spread created a massive AMT obligation."

Olivia felt panic rising in her chest.

"But most of my money is still in stock."

"I know," Mark replied quietly.

At first she assumed the situation would resolve itself because Apex stock continued rising temporarily. Yet several months later, the technology market shifted dramatically. Interest rates increased. Investors began pulling back from growth stocks. Apex missed quarterly expectations slightly.

The stock collapsed nearly 45% over the next year.

Olivia watched helplessly as her paper fortune shrank while the enormous tax bill remained.

For weeks she barely slept.

She considered selling shares aggressively, but insider restrictions complicated timing. Meanwhile, state and federal tax deadlines approached rapidly. Financial headlines that once praised Apex now criticized the company relentlessly.

One evening Olivia sat alone in her apartment surrounded by tax documents and market reports. She felt emotionally exhausted.

"How did I become rich and terrified at the same time?" she whispered aloud.

The next morning she contacted a sophisticated wealth management attorney recommended by another executive.

His name was David Mercer.

After reviewing her situation carefully, David leaned back thoughtfully.

"You're not the first founder or executive this has happened to," he explained. "And you won't be the last."

Olivia sighed. "I thought making money would simplify life."

David smiled slightly. "Large wealth makes planning more important, not less."

Over the next year, David and his advisory team helped Olivia completely restructure her financial strategy. They created a systematic diversification plan tied to future vesting and trading windows. They established charitable giving structures using appreciated stock. They implemented tax-loss harvesting strategies across portions of her portfolio. Olivia relocated officially to Florida to reduce future state tax exposure. Trust structures were established for long-term estate planning. Most importantly, every future liquidity decision became coordinated through a comprehensive tax framework instead of emotional reactions.

The transformation changed not only Olivia's finances but also her mindset.

Before, she viewed taxes as an annoying afterthought. Now she understood taxation as one of the largest determinants of long-term wealth preservation.

Several years later, Apex Quantum recovered partially and stabilized as a successful public company. Olivia's diversified portfolio, however, no longer depended entirely on Apex's stock performance. She owned real estate investments, dividend portfolios, private businesses, and conservative income-producing assets alongside her remaining shares.

More importantly, she regained peace of mind.

During a conference for startup executives, a young employee approached her nervously after a panel discussion.

"I just received stock options at my company," he said. "What's the biggest mistake people make after an IPO?"

Olivia smiled knowingly.

"They spend years learning how to build wealth," she replied. "But almost no one teaches them how to keep it."

Chapter 4

Liquidity Events, Lockup Periods, and Strategic Stock Selling

One of the most emotionally intense phases after a company goes public involves managing liquidity events and stock sales. For founders, executives, employees, and early investors, the IPO creates the possibility of transforming years of illiquid equity into usable financial capital. Yet this transition is rarely immediate or simple. Newly public shareholders often imagine the IPO as a moment when wealth suddenly becomes accessible, but the reality is far more complex. Lockup agreements, insider trading rules, tax implications, market volatility, investor perception, and emotional decision-making all shape how and when shares can be sold. Understanding liquidity management becomes essential because the decisions made during this period can permanently influence long-term financial outcomes.

Liquidity itself is one of the defining differences between private and public markets. Before an IPO, company ownership is typically difficult to sell. Shares are privately held, valuations may be uncertain, and transactions are restricted. After an IPO, however, shares become tradable on public exchanges where prices fluctuate constantly based on supply, demand, investor sentiment, and market conditions. This transformation creates opportunity, but it also introduces psychological pressure unlike anything most founders have previously experienced.

The first major concept newly public shareholders must understand is the lockup period. Most IPOs include contractual lockup agreements that prevent insiders from selling shares for a certain period after the public offering, commonly around 90 to 180 days. These restrictions exist because investment banks and institutional investors want to avoid massive insider selling immediately after the IPO, which could destabilize the stock price and damage investor confidence. While lockups protect market stability, they also create frustration for many shareholders who suddenly appear wealthy but remain unable to access much of their capital.

During lockup periods, emotions often intensify dramatically. If the stock price rises rapidly after the IPO, insiders may feel excitement mixed with anxiety because they cannot immediately capture gains. Conversely, if the stock declines significantly before the lockup expires, shareholders may feel trapped watching paper wealth evaporate without the ability to act. This emotional volatility can lead to poor decision-making once restrictions are finally lifted. The expiration of a lockup period often becomes a major event in public markets.

Investors and analysts closely monitor insider behavior because stock sales by founders and executives may influence market perception. Large insider selling can sometimes signal reduced confidence in future growth, even when sales are motivated purely by diversification or tax planning. As a result, strategic communication and gradual selling often become important components of liquidity management.

Many founders initially struggle emotionally with the idea of selling shares. They spent years building the company and often associate ownership with personal identity, loyalty, and conviction. Selling stock may feel psychologically uncomfortable, almost like abandoning the business they sacrificed so much to create. Yet refusing to sell any shares creates concentration risk that can threaten long-term financial security. The challenge becomes balancing emotional attachment with rational financial planning.

One of the most dangerous mistakes shareholders make after lockup expiration is attempting to time the market perfectly. Some individuals become obsessed with maximizing every possible dollar by predicting short-term stock movements. They delay diversification repeatedly because they believe the stock will continue climbing. Others panic during temporary declines and sell aggressively out of fear. Both extremes are usually driven by emotion rather than disciplined planning.

Sophisticated liquidity management typically focuses less on predicting market tops and more on creating structured systems. Many successful founders establish predetermined selling frameworks that gradually reduce concentrated exposure over time. Instead of relying on emotional instincts, they follow disciplined plans designed around long-term financial goals, tax efficiency, and risk management.

Rule 10b5-1 trading plans have become one of the most important tools for executives managing public company stock sales. These plans allow insiders to establish predetermined schedules for future trades while not possessing material nonpublic information. Once the plan is implemented, shares may be sold automatically according to specified conditions. This structure helps executives avoid accusations of insider trading while reducing emotional decision-making during periods of market volatility.

The psychological benefits of systematic selling are often underestimated. Public markets create constant emotional temptation. Rising stock prices generate greed and overconfidence, while declining prices trigger fear and regret. Structured liquidity plans help remove emotion from the process by replacing reactive behavior with disciplined execution. Over time, this consistency often produces better financial outcomes than attempting to outguess short-term market movements.

Taxation also plays a critical role in liquidity strategy. Selling shares creates taxable events, and the timing of those sales can dramatically influence after-tax wealth. Long-term capital gains rates are generally more favorable than short-term rates, encouraging some shareholders to hold positions longer before selling. However, tax optimization should never completely override risk management considerations. Holding excessively concentrated positions purely to avoid taxes may expose wealth to far greater losses during market downturns.

Some founders use staged liquidity strategies designed to balance diversification with continued upside participation. For example, they may sell a fixed percentage of shares annually while retaining meaningful ownership positions. Others use collars, prepaid variable forwards, exchange funds, or hedging strategies to reduce downside exposure while delaying immediate taxation. These advanced techniques often require sophisticated legal and financial guidance but can provide flexibility during post-IPO transitions.

Another important aspect of liquidity management involves understanding personal cash flow needs. Many founders become wealthy on paper while remaining surprisingly illiquid. Their wealth may exist almost entirely in stock, leaving limited access to cash for taxes, investments, lifestyle needs, or future opportunities. Strategic stock sales therefore help create practical financial flexibility rather than simply theoretical net worth.

Liquidity events also introduce social and psychological pressures. Newly wealthy individuals often face increased requests for financial support, investments, business opportunities, and personal loans. Family dynamics may shift. Friendships may change. Public visibility can create expectations that become emotionally exhausting. Establishing boundaries and financial discipline becomes essential because sudden wealth can disappear quickly when spending and obligations expand too aggressively.

Lifestyle inflation represents another major danger after liquidity events. During rising markets, shareholders often assume future stock appreciation will continue indefinitely. This belief encourages larger homes, luxury purchases, speculative investments, and escalating monthly expenses. However, markets are cyclical. Stock prices fluctuate. Founders who tie permanent lifestyle obligations to temporary valuation peaks may experience severe financial stress during downturns.

The most financially resilient individuals often adopt surprisingly conservative approaches after major liquidity events. Rather than maximizing visible consumption, they prioritize stability, flexibility, and long-term security. They maintain liquidity reserves, reduce leverage, diversify income streams, and build portfolios designed to survive multiple economic cycles. This discipline may appear less glamorous publicly, but it significantly improves long-term wealth preservation.

Another challenge after an IPO involves balancing personal financial goals with leadership responsibilities. Public company executives understand that insider selling may influence employee morale and investor confidence. Employees often monitor executive transactions closely, interpreting large sales as signals about future company performance. Effective communication therefore becomes important. Founders who explain diversification strategies transparently may reduce unnecessary speculation or concern.

Many founders also struggle emotionally because liquidity changes their relationship with work itself. Before an IPO, financial necessity often drives relentless focus and ambition. After achieving substantial wealth, motivation becomes more complicated. Some founders lose intensity because survival pressure disappears. Others continue working obsessively despite already achieving financial independence. Managing liquidity therefore involves not only financial transitions but also identity transitions. One important lesson repeated throughout financial history is that unrealized wealth can disappear quickly. Bull markets create confidence that rising valuations will continue forever, but economic cycles inevitably shift. Companies once considered unstoppable can decline dramatically due to changing industries, competition, regulation, technological disruption, or broader recessions. Liquidity events provide opportunities to convert volatile equity into durable financial security before conditions change unexpectedly.

The timing of major liquidity events often intersects with broader macroeconomic conditions. During periods of low interest rates and strong investor optimism, valuations may rise rapidly. During tightening cycles or economic contractions, liquidity opportunities may become more limited. While predicting markets precisely is impossible, understanding broader economic cycles helps founders contextualize risk exposure and avoid unrealistic assumptions.

Family wealth planning frequently accelerates after liquidity events as well. Once shares become marketable, many individuals begin focusing more seriously on trusts, charitable planning, estate structures, and multi-generational financial strategies. Liquidity creates opportunities not only for personal freedom but also for long-term family impact. Wealth preservation increasingly becomes about stewardship rather than accumulation alone.

Another overlooked aspect of liquidity management is emotional adaptation. Sudden wealth changes how individuals perceive risk, opportunity, relationships, and personal identity. Some founders become excessively fearful after achieving financial success because they worry about losing it. Others become reckless because rising valuations distort risk perception. Sustainable wealth management requires emotional balance and long-term perspective rather than reactive behavior.

The most successful post-IPO shareholders often share one important characteristic: they treat liquidity as a process rather than a single event. They understand that wealth management evolves over years, not days. They focus less on maximizing short-term stock prices and more on building enduring financial systems capable of surviving uncertainty. Their goal is not merely becoming wealthy, but remaining financially secure regardless of future market conditions.

Ultimately, liquidity events represent moments of enormous opportunity and enormous responsibility. The ability to convert concentrated equity into diversified financial independence is one of the defining advantages of public markets. Yet achieving that transition successfully requires discipline, planning, humility, and emotional maturity. Lockup expirations, stock sales, and liquidity management are not merely technical financial events—they are turning points that shape whether temporary paper wealth becomes permanent financial freedom.

The Lockup Expiration That Tested Marcus Bennett

Marcus Bennett could barely sleep during the final weeks before Vertex Dynamics went public.

For nearly twelve years, he had devoted his life to building the cybersecurity company from a tiny startup into one of the fastest-growing technology firms in the country. The journey had nearly destroyed him emotionally more than once. There were years of constant fundraising pressure, failed product launches, employee turnover, and moments when bankruptcy seemed unavoidable.

Now everything had changed.

Vertex Dynamics was preparing for one of the biggest IPOs of the year.

On listing day, Marcus stood beside executives and investment bankers on the exchange floor while cameras flashed around them. Employees watching remotely cried with excitement as the stock opened nearly 50% above its offering price.

By the end of the trading day, Marcus's shares were worth over $860 million. The media frenzy became immediate.

Business magazines called him a visionary founder. Podcasts invited him for interviews. Venture capital firms treated him like royalty. His social media exploded with messages from strangers congratulating him.

But despite the headlines, Marcus quickly discovered something strange.

He was rich, but he could not actually touch most of the money.

The IPO lockup agreement prevented insiders from selling shares for six months. During that period, Vertex stock continued climbing aggressively. Every week Marcus's paper fortune increased further. Analysts predicted the company would dominate cybersecurity markets for years.

His friends constantly joked about his growing net worth.

"You're almost a billionaire now," one friend laughed during dinner.

Marcus smiled politely, but internally he felt trapped. Nearly all his wealth remained tied to one stock. He could not diversify yet. He could not reduce risk. He could only watch the market move daily.

At first the rising price felt exhilarating.

Then it became psychologically exhausting.

Every morning Marcus checked Vertex's stock before getting out of bed. Good market days made him euphoric. Red days made him anxious. His emotional state became completely connected to market fluctuations.

His financial advisor, Laura Kim, noticed the change immediately.

"You need a plan before the lockup expires," she told him during one meeting.

Marcus shrugged. "Why sell? The company's stronger than ever."

Laura leaned forward carefully. "That's exactly why you should think strategically now."

Marcus frowned. "Selling feels wrong."

"Diversifying isn't betrayal," she replied calmly. "It's survival."

But Marcus resisted.

He believed deeply in Vertex. Selling shares felt emotionally impossible after sacrificing so much to build the company. Besides, analysts kept raising price targets. The stock seemed unstoppable. As lockup expiration approached, media speculation intensified. Financial journalists debated whether insiders would sell aggressively. Investors watched executive filings closely.

The night before the lockup ended, Marcus sat alone in his office overlooking downtown San Francisco.

He opened several spreadsheets Laura had prepared for him weeks earlier. One scenario showed what his finances could look like if he diversified gradually into multiple asset classes. Another showed what would happen if Vertex stock experienced a severe downturn while remaining highly concentrated.

The numbers unsettled him.

Still, he hesitated.

"What if the stock doubles again?" he thought.

The next morning Laura called him early.

"You don't need to sell everything," she said. "But you do need to protect your future."

Marcus stared silently at the city skyline.

For the first time, he realized something important.

He had spent his entire adult life learning how to take risk. Now he needed to learn how to manage it. Over the next several weeks, Marcus implemented a structured liquidity strategy. Through a Rule 10b5-1 plan, he gradually sold portions of his holdings on predetermined schedules. The process felt emotionally painful at first. Every sale triggered anxiety that he might miss future gains.

Then the market changed unexpectedly.

Several months later, a major economic slowdown hit technology markets. Interest rates rose sharply. Investor sentiment collapsed. High-growth stocks across the sector fell aggressively.

Vertex Dynamics dropped nearly 55% from its peak within one year.

Employees panicked. Financial media turned negative. Some executives who had refused to diversify lost hundreds of millions of dollars in paper wealth.

Marcus watched the decline carefully from his office one evening.

Oddly, he felt calm.

Because of his structured liquidity strategy, much of his wealth had already been diversified into real estate, bonds, dividend portfolios, and cash reserves. While Vertex still represented an important part of his net worth, his financial future no longer depended entirely on one stock chart.

For the first time since the IPO, he felt emotionally free.

Months later, Marcus spoke privately with a young founder preparing for her own IPO.

She looked nervous.

"How do you know when to sell?" she asked.

Marcus smiled thoughtfully.

"You don't wait until you stop believing in the company," he said quietly. "You sell because you believe your future deserves protection too."

Chapter 5

Building a Family Office and Long-Term Wealth Preservation System

For many founders, executives, and early investors, the period following an IPO marks the first time they must think beyond wealth creation and begin focusing seriously on wealth preservation. During the startup phase, nearly all energy revolves around survival, growth, fundraising, hiring, product development, and scaling operations. Financial complexity remains relatively narrow because the business itself dominates every major decision. After a liquidity event, however, life changes dramatically. Suddenly, the entrepreneur who once focused exclusively on growing one company may now oversee hundreds of millions—or even billions—of dollars spread across investments, taxes, trusts, insurance structures, charitable planning, real estate holdings, and family financial responsibilities. This transition often creates the need for a completely new financial infrastructure: the family office.

A family office is not simply an investment account or financial advisor relationship. At its core, a family office is a centralized system designed to manage, preserve, protect, and grow significant wealth across generations. It integrates investment management, tax strategy, legal planning, estate structures, philanthropy, risk management, accounting, governance, and family education into one coordinated framework. While ultra-wealthy families have used these structures for generations, many modern technology founders and entrepreneurs are now entering wealth levels where family office strategies become increasingly relevant after IPOs and liquidity events.

One of the first realities wealthy founders encounter is that substantial wealth creates complexity. Before becoming wealthy, most financial decisions are relatively straightforward. Income is earned through salary or business profits, taxes are filed annually, and investments may be limited to retirement accounts or a few simple assets. After a major liquidity event, however, financial responsibilities expand rapidly. Public equity positions, private investments, real estate portfolios, venture capital exposure, charitable foundations, trusts, tax jurisdictions, insurance structures, and succession planning all begin interacting simultaneously. Without organized systems, wealth becomes vulnerable to inefficiency, conflict, taxation, mismanagement, and emotional decision-making.

The purpose of a family office is not merely to increase returns. Its primary purpose is to create coordination and continuity. Wealth preservation requires organization. It requires professionals who understand how investment strategy, taxation, estate planning, insurance, philanthropy, and legal structures work together over decades. The family office acts as the operational center for long-term wealth stewardship.

Family offices generally fall into two categories: single-family offices and multi-family offices. A single-family office serves one wealthy family exclusively and often includes dedicated in-house employees such as investment managers, accountants, attorneys, tax specialists, estate planners, and administrative staff. These structures provide maximum customization and privacy but require substantial wealth to operate efficiently. Multi-family offices, on the other hand, serve multiple wealthy families simultaneously, allowing clients to access sophisticated expertise without bearing the full operational cost of building an independent organization.

Many newly wealthy founders initially resist the idea of creating formal wealth management systems because entrepreneurial culture often emphasizes independence and lean operations. Entrepreneurs are accustomed to controlling costs, moving quickly, and making decisions personally. However, as wealth grows, unmanaged complexity becomes dangerous. Even small mistakes involving taxes, legal structures, asset protection, or succession planning can cost millions over time. Sophisticated systems become increasingly valuable as financial scale expands. One of the most important functions of a family office is investment management and portfolio coordination. After an IPO, founders often hold concentrated positions in company stock alongside growing cash reserves and alternative investments. Without strategic oversight, portfolios can become fragmented, overly risky, tax inefficient, or emotionally driven. Family offices help create disciplined asset allocation frameworks designed around long-term objectives rather than short-term market emotions.

Diversification becomes especially important at this stage. Many founders spent years building wealth through concentrated entrepreneurial risk. Yet preserving wealth often requires a different mindset entirely. Public equities, private businesses, bonds, real estate, infrastructure assets, private credit, venture capital, commodities, and international investments may all play roles within sophisticated family office portfolios. The objective is not merely maximizing returns but balancing growth, stability, liquidity, inflation protection, and downside risk management.

Another major role of family offices involves tax coordination. Wealthy individuals face increasingly complex tax obligations across investment income, capital gains, trusts, estate transfers, charitable giving, business ownership, and international exposure. Tax planning therefore becomes integrated into nearly every financial decision. Family offices often work closely with legal and accounting professionals to structure transactions efficiently while adapting to changing tax laws over time.

Estate planning also becomes central to long-term wealth preservation. Many entrepreneurs initially focus almost entirely on personal financial success but eventually realize that wealth transfer across generations requires intentional planning. Without proper structures, estate taxes, legal disputes, poor governance, and family conflict can rapidly erode financial legacies. History contains countless examples of great fortunes disappearing within only a few generations due to inadequate planning and weak financial stewardship.

Trusts often become foundational components of family office structures. Dynasty trusts, generation-skipping trusts, charitable trusts, grantor retained annuity trusts, and family limited partnerships may all help preserve assets while reducing future tax exposure. These structures also provide governance mechanisms that define how wealth will be managed and distributed over time. Effective estate planning is not simply about minimizing taxes—it is about creating continuity, responsibility, and long-term family stability.

Philanthropy also plays a major role within many family offices. After achieving financial success, many founders begin focusing more seriously on impact, legacy, and purpose. Charitable foundations, donor-advised funds, educational initiatives, healthcare programs, environmental projects, and social impact investing often become important components of wealth strategy. Family offices help coordinate these initiatives while integrating philanthropic goals into broader tax and estate planning frameworks.

Risk management is another critical function often overlooked by newly wealthy individuals. As wealth grows, exposure to lawsuits, cyber threats, reputational risk, business liabilities, and personal security concerns increases substantially. Family offices frequently coordinate insurance structures, legal asset protection strategies, cybersecurity systems, and privacy protocols designed to reduce these risks. Wealth preservation requires protecting not only assets themselves but also the systems surrounding those assets.

Real estate management also becomes increasingly important after liquidity events. Many wealthy founders accumulate residential properties, investment real estate, vacation homes, agricultural land, or commercial holdings across multiple jurisdictions. Family offices help oversee financing, operations, taxes, maintenance, staffing, insurance, and legal coordination related to these assets. Without centralized management, real estate portfolios can become inefficient and difficult to administer. One of the most underestimated aspects of family office planning involves education and family governance. Wealth transfer often fails not because assets disappear immediately, but because future generations are unprepared to manage responsibility. Studies repeatedly show that many family fortunes decline significantly by the second or third generation due to poor communication, lack of financial literacy, entitlement, internal conflict, or absence of shared purpose.

Sophisticated families therefore invest heavily in educating children and heirs about financial stewardship, investing, entrepreneurship, philanthropy, and governance. Family meetings, investment education programs, mentorship systems, and clearly defined governance structures help create continuity across generations. Wealth preservation ultimately depends not only on financial assets but also on the values and behaviors surrounding those assets.

Many entrepreneurs experience psychological difficulty transitioning from aggressive business builders into long-term wealth stewards. During the startup phase, rapid decision-making and high-risk behavior are often rewarded. After major liquidity events, however, preserving wealth frequently requires patience, discipline, delegation, and long-term planning. Some founders continue taking excessive risks because they feel emotionally uncomfortable shifting away from entrepreneurial intensity. Others struggle with identity because wealth changes their relationship with ambition and work.

The family office framework helps create structure during this transition. Instead of making reactive emotional decisions, founders begin operating within organized systems guided by long-term objectives. Wealth management becomes less about daily market fluctuations and more about strategic continuity over decades.

Privacy and discretion also become increasingly important after an IPO. Public visibility often increases dramatically following major liquidity events. Wealthy individuals may face security concerns, media attention, aggressive sales pitches, investment scams, or unwanted public exposure. Family offices frequently coordinate confidentiality measures, legal protections, and operational structures designed to preserve privacy and reduce vulnerability.

Another important aspect of family office strategy is liquidity planning. Wealth preservation requires maintaining appropriate cash reserves and financial flexibility during market cycles. Some wealthy individuals become overexposed to illiquid assets such as private equity, venture investments, or real estate, leaving insufficient liquidity during downturns or emergencies. Family offices help balance long-term growth opportunities with liquidity needs and operational stability.

Technology and data management have also become increasingly important within modern family offices. Sophisticated reporting systems, consolidated investment tracking, cybersecurity protocols, document management, tax coordination software, and communication infrastructure help wealthy families manage increasingly complex financial ecosystems efficiently.

Importantly, building a family office does not require billionaire status. Many family office principles can benefit individuals with far lower net worth levels. The underlying philosophy is organization, intentionality, and long-term coordination. Whether managing $10 million or $1 billion, structured systems significantly improve wealth preservation outcomes compared to fragmented, reactive decision-making.

One of the most valuable lessons successful families understand is that wealth preservation is an ongoing process rather than a one-time achievement. Economic cycles change. Tax laws evolve. Markets fluctuate. Family dynamics shift over time. Effective family offices therefore remain adaptable while maintaining long-term strategic discipline.

Ultimately, the purpose of wealth extends beyond accumulation alone. Financial success creates opportunities for freedom, security, impact, education, philanthropy, and generational stability. Yet these outcomes rarely happen automatically. Without structure, coordination, and intentional stewardship, even extraordinary fortunes can disappear surprisingly quickly.

The transition from entrepreneur to wealth steward represents one of the most important psychological shifts after an IPO. Building a company may create wealth, but building systems determines whether that wealth survives across generations. The family office exists not merely to manage money, but to protect vision, continuity, values, and long-term opportunity for decades to come.

How Sophia Ramirez Built a Family Office That Protected Her Legacy

Sophia Ramirez never imagined she would one day oversee more money than she could count comfortably in her head.

For most of her life, money had represented survival.

She grew up in a small apartment in Phoenix where her parents worked multiple jobs to support the family. Her father repaired air conditioning systems during brutal Arizona summers, while her mother cleaned hotel rooms late into the night. Sophia learned early that financial security was fragile. Bills mattered. Debt mattered. Every dollar mattered. Those lessons stayed with her long after she became successful.

At twenty-eight, Sophia launched a cloud logistics software company called AxisFlow with two former engineering coworkers. During the early years, the company nearly failed several times. Investors rejected them repeatedly. Payroll problems became common. Sophia maxed out credit cards to keep operations alive.

But eventually the company broke through.

Major retail corporations adopted AxisFlow's software platform, and revenue exploded globally. Within eight years, the company became one of the fastest-growing logistics technology firms in the world.

When AxisFlow went public, Sophia's ownership stake was suddenly worth nearly $640 million.

The number felt impossible.

At first, she handled the wealth transition casually. She hired a financial advisor, opened several investment accounts, and purchased homes in Scottsdale and Miami. But within two years, her financial life became increasingly chaotic.

Investment statements arrived from dozens of different accounts. Venture capital firms constantly pitched startup opportunities. Tax documents became overwhelming. Family members requested loans and business funding. Attorneys discussed trusts she barely understood. Insurance agents recommended complicated asset protection structures. Private bankers proposed sophisticated investment products she did not fully trust.

One evening Sophia sat alone at her kitchen table surrounded by stacks of paperwork.

For the first time since the IPO, she felt completely overwhelmed.

"I built a company," she whispered to herself. "But I have no idea how to manage this."

The breaking point came during a tense meeting with her accountant.

After reviewing several years of financial activity, he looked up seriously.

"You have no centralized coordination," he explained. "Your investments, taxes, legal structures, and estate planning are all disconnected."

Sophia frowned. "What does that mean?"

"It means complexity is starting to control you instead of the other way around." Those words stayed with her.

A few weeks later, Sophia met Daniel Kessler, a veteran advisor who specialized in family office structures for entrepreneurs after liquidity events.

During their first meeting, Daniel asked her a simple question.

"What do you actually want your wealth to accomplish?"

Sophia paused silently.

No one had ever asked her that before.

Most advisors focused on returns, taxes, or investments. But Daniel wanted to understand her vision.

After a long silence, Sophia finally answered.

"I want freedom," she said quietly. "And I want my family to never experience the instability I grew up with."

Daniel nodded.

"Then you don't just need investments," he said. "You need a system."

Over the following year, Sophia built a sophisticated family office structure around her wealth.

At first the process felt intimidating. Attorneys established trusts and governance documents. Investment professionals consolidated scattered portfolios into coordinated asset allocation strategies. Tax advisors restructured entities and charitable planning systems. Cybersecurity experts protected sensitive financial information. Real estate managers organized property oversight.

Slowly, the chaos disappeared.

For the first time since the IPO, Sophia felt clarity returning.

Her family office diversified her holdings beyond AxisFlow stock into income-producing real estate, infrastructure investments, private equity, fixed income, and dividend portfolios. Liquidity reserves were established for economic downturns. Charitable foundations funded educational scholarships for low-income engineering students. Family governance meetings were created to educate younger relatives about financial responsibility and stewardship.

Most importantly, Sophia's relationship with money changed emotionally.

Before, wealth felt stressful and unstable despite its size. Every investment decision triggered anxiety. Every market downturn felt personal.

Now she understood something deeper. True wealth was not merely about numbers on financial statements. True wealth was about systems that created long-term resilience and peace of mind.

Several years later, during a private family retreat in Colorado, Sophia sat beside her teenage nephew overlooking the mountains at sunset.

"Are you ever afraid of losing everything?" he asked quietly.

Sophia smiled thoughtfully.

"I used to be," she admitted.

"What changed?"

She looked toward the horizon before answering.

"I realized wealth isn't protected by luck," she said softly. "It's protected by preparation."

Chapter 6

Psychological Challenges of Sudden Wealth and Post-IPO Identity Shifts

One of the most underestimated aspects of going public is the psychological transformation that follows major liquidity events. Most discussions surrounding IPOs focus heavily on valuations, stock performance, wealth creation, taxes, and financial strategy. Yet behind the financial headlines lies a far more personal reality. Sudden wealth changes how individuals think, feel, behave, and relate to the world around them. Founders, executives, and early employees often spend years imagining that financial success will solve stress and create permanent happiness, only to discover that wealth introduces entirely new emotional challenges they never anticipated.

The transition from struggling entrepreneur to wealthy public shareholder is not merely financial—it is deeply psychological. During the startup phase, life is often structured around survival, ambition, sacrifice, and relentless forward momentum. Entrepreneurs wake up each day focused on solving urgent problems. The company becomes the center of personal identity. Every challenge feels meaningful because the stakes are existential. Founders often endure years of uncertainty, financial instability, emotional pressure, and social sacrifice while pursuing their vision.

Then, suddenly, everything changes.

After an IPO, the same founder who once worried about payroll and investor meetings may now possess more wealth than they ever imagined possible. Yet surprisingly, this financial success often creates emotional confusion rather than clarity. Many individuals experience a profound psychological disconnect between external success and internal fulfillment. They discover that wealth changes circumstances quickly, but emotional patterns, fears, insecurities, and personal identity do not automatically transform alongside bank accounts.

One of the first psychological challenges after sudden wealth is identity disruption. For years, many entrepreneurs define themselves almost entirely through struggle and ambition. Their self-worth becomes deeply connected to building the company, overcoming obstacles, and chasing growth. The startup journey provides constant urgency and purpose. When financial freedom finally arrives, some founders feel emotionally disoriented because the identity that drove them for years suddenly loses its structure.

This phenomenon is more common than most people realize. Founders often believe they are pursuing money, but in reality they are also pursuing meaning, validation, achievement, control, or personal significance. Once wealth removes financial pressure, deeper emotional questions emerge. Who am I beyond the company? What motivates me now? What does success actually mean? What am I trying to build next? These questions can create anxiety, emptiness, or restlessness even in individuals who appear extraordinarily successful publicly.

Another major psychological challenge involves the sudden shift in social dynamics. Wealth changes relationships. Friends, family members, business contacts, and even strangers may begin treating wealthy individuals differently after an IPO. Some relationships become transactional. Others become complicated by envy, expectations, or financial dependency. Founders who once felt socially invisible may suddenly become highly visible due to media attention, public recognition, or financial status.

This visibility often creates emotional isolation. Many wealthy individuals quietly wonder whether people genuinely value them as individuals or simply value their financial success. Invitations increase. Opportunities multiply. Compliments become constant. Yet authentic trust may become harder to identify. Some founders become emotionally guarded because they fear exploitation or manipulation. Others overspend or over-give financially in attempts to maintain relationships and avoid guilt surrounding their success. Family relationships may also shift dramatically after liquidity events. Parents who once worried about a founder's risky entrepreneurial choices may suddenly treat them differently. Siblings may experience jealousy or insecurity. Extended family members may request financial support, investments, or business opportunities. Wealth can amplify existing family dynamics while introducing new emotional tension surrounding responsibility, expectations, and fairness.

Guilt becomes another surprisingly common emotion after sudden wealth creation. Some founders experience "wealth guilt," particularly if they grew up in financially difficult environments or achieved success while others around them continued struggling. They may feel uncomfortable spending money, discussing success publicly, or setting financial boundaries with friends and family. Others feel pressure to solve everyone's problems because their financial capacity appears limitless from the outside.

At the same time, some individuals experience the opposite reaction: overconfidence and emotional excess. Sudden wealth can distort risk perception dramatically. Bull markets and rapidly rising stock prices create feelings of invincibility. Founders who succeeded in business may begin believing their judgment is superior across all areas of life, leading to reckless investments, excessive spending, or poor personal decisions. Financial success in one field does not automatically create wisdom in every domain, yet wealth often creates the illusion of universal competence.

Lifestyle inflation becomes one of the most visible psychological traps after an IPO. During the startup phase, many entrepreneurs delay gratification for years. They dream about future freedom, luxury, and financial flexibility. Once liquidity arrives, there is often a strong emotional temptation to reward years of sacrifice through aggressive spending. Expensive homes, luxury cars, private travel, social status purchases, and speculative investments may quickly follow.

Initially, these upgrades feel exciting. Yet research repeatedly shows that material consumption creates only temporary emotional satisfaction. Over time, elevated lifestyles become normalized, and happiness levels often return to previous baselines. Meanwhile, large financial obligations create pressure and reduce flexibility during future market downturns. Many wealthy individuals eventually discover that freedom comes less from consumption and more from simplicity, optionality, and emotional stability.

The volatility of public markets also creates unique psychological pressure after an IPO. In private companies, valuations may update only occasionally during funding rounds. In public markets, however, net worth fluctuates constantly in real time. A founder's wealth may rise or fall by millions of dollars within a single trading day based on earnings reports, economic news, analyst opinions, or market sentiment.

This visibility can become emotionally addictive. Some founders obsessively monitor stock prices throughout the day, allowing short-term market movements to control mood and self-esteem. Positive stock performance creates euphoria, while declines create fear, anger, or self-doubt. Over time, this emotional dependency becomes exhausting and psychologically unhealthy.

Another major challenge after financial success is loss of urgency. During the startup phase, survival pressure often creates intense focus and productivity. Entrepreneurs push themselves relentlessly because failure carries serious consequences. After achieving financial freedom, however, some founders struggle with motivation because the stakes feel different. Without financial necessity driving ambition, they may feel directionless or emotionally flat.

This explains why many successful entrepreneurs continue launching companies even after becoming wealthy. The process itself—not merely the money—often provides meaning, challenge, and identity. Building something meaningful satisfies emotional needs that wealth alone cannot replace. However, some founders fail to recognize this distinction and continue chasing increasingly larger financial goals believing another milestone will finally create fulfillment.

Hedonic adaptation also plays a significant role in post-IPO psychology. Human beings quickly adjust to improved circumstances. The excitement of wealth, luxury, or status tends to fade faster than expected. What once felt extraordinary gradually becomes ordinary. This adaptation can create an endless cycle of chasing larger achievements, higher valuations, or greater wealth without experiencing lasting satisfaction.

Some founders become trapped in constant comparison after an IPO. Public markets create visible rankings of wealth, valuations, and financial performance. Entrepreneurs who once felt successful may suddenly compare themselves against billionaires, hedge fund managers, or founders with larger exits. Social media and financial media amplify this comparison culture constantly. As a result, individuals with extraordinary wealth may still feel inadequate relative to others.

Mental health challenges also become more visible after liquidity events. Anxiety, depression, burnout, loneliness, substance abuse, and emotional exhaustion are surprisingly common among high-performing entrepreneurs. The pressure to maintain success publicly while navigating complex emotional transitions privately can become overwhelming. Unfortunately, many founders avoid seeking help because society assumes wealth eliminates emotional struggle.

In reality, psychological resilience becomes increasingly important as financial complexity grows. Therapy, mentorship, mindfulness practices, physical health routines, strong personal relationships, and emotional self-awareness all become essential components of long-term well-being. Sustainable success requires managing not only money, but also mindset and emotional health.

Purpose becomes one of the most important long-term questions after financial independence. Once survival and financial security are achieved, individuals must decide what truly matters moving forward. Some founders turn toward philanthropy, mentorship, education, investing, or social impact initiatives. Others focus on family, health, spirituality, creativity, or personal development. The healthiest transitions often occur when wealth becomes a tool supporting deeper values rather than the sole objective itself.

One of the most powerful realizations many wealthy individuals eventually reach is that money amplifies identity rather than replacing it. Wealth provides options, flexibility, and opportunities, but it does not automatically create happiness, meaning, or emotional peace. Individuals who lacked emotional balance before wealth often continue struggling afterward, only now with greater complexity surrounding them.

This is why intentional self-awareness becomes so important after an IPO. Founders who understand their emotional patterns, insecurities, motivations, and psychological vulnerabilities are far more likely to navigate wealth transitions successfully. Emotional maturity becomes just as valuable as financial intelligence.

Ultimately, the goal of post-IPO life should not merely be financial success. The deeper objective is creating a sustainable relationship between wealth, purpose, identity, and well-being. Wealth can create freedom, but freedom itself requires direction. Without emotional grounding and meaningful purpose, even extraordinary financial success may feel strangely empty over time.

The IPO may transform a founder's bank account overnight, but building a fulfilling life afterward requires something much deeper than money alone. It requires emotional clarity, intentionality, balance, and the willingness to redefine success beyond public valuation metrics. In the end, lasting fulfillment comes not from how much wealth is created, but from how wisely that wealth is integrated into a meaningful life.

The Empty Penthouse and the Billion-Dollar Question

When Adrian Wells stood on the balcony of his Manhattan penthouse overlooking the city skyline, he realized something deeply unsettling.

He felt completely empty.

Just eighteen months earlier, Adrian had become one of the youngest technology billionaires in the country after his AI software company, NeuroLink Systems, went public. Financial media celebrated him endlessly. Magazine covers called him a genius entrepreneur. Investors praised his vision. Social media treated him like a celebrity.

At thirty-six years old, his net worth had surpassed $1.3 billion on paper.

Yet standing there alone at midnight in one of the most expensive apartments in New York City, Adrian felt more disconnected than ever.

The strange part was that everything looked successful from the outside.

The IPO had exceeded every expectation. NeuroLink's stock surged nearly 85% during its first year as a public company. Adrian purchased luxury properties in Manhattan and Malibu. He traveled privately. Elite investors invited him into exclusive circles. Famous athletes and entertainers suddenly wanted friendships with him.

But internally, something had shifted after the IPO.

For more than a decade, Adrian's entire identity revolved around building NeuroLink. Every morning carried urgency. Every problem mattered. Every challenge created purpose. During the startup years, survival pressure fueled him constantly. There was always another investor meeting, product launch, hiring decision, or funding crisis demanding his attention.

Then, almost overnight, financial survival disappeared.

At first, Adrian thought this freedom would feel euphoric forever.

Instead, it slowly created emotional confusion.

He found himself checking NeuroLink's stock price obsessively throughout the day. When shares climbed, he felt powerful. When the stock dropped, anxiety consumed him. His emotional state became completely tied to market fluctuations.

At the same time, relationships around him changed dramatically.

Friends who once ignored his startup suddenly praised him constantly. Family members requested financial help for business ventures. Strangers treated him differently at restaurants, conferences, and events. Women seemed more interested in his wealth than his personality. Every interaction began feeling transactional.

One evening during a private dinner in Los Angeles, Adrian sat surrounded by celebrities, venture capitalists, and executives laughing over expensive wine.

Yet internally he felt strangely detached.

He realized he trusted almost no one at the table.

Several months later, the emotional pressure intensified further when NeuroLink's stock became volatile during a technology market correction. Adrian's net worth fluctuated by hundreds of millions of dollars within weeks. News headlines praised him one day and criticized him the next.

Sleep became difficult.

Despite having extraordinary wealth, Adrian constantly felt restless and anxious.

One afternoon his older sister Elena visited him unexpectedly.

She walked slowly through the massive penthouse before sitting across from him near the floor-to-ceiling windows.

"You don't seem happy," she said quietly.

Adrian laughed uncomfortably. "I'm a billionaire, Elena."

"That's not what I asked."

Her words lingered painfully in the silence.

For the first time, Adrian admitted something to himself he had avoided for months.

He had spent his entire adult life chasing success without ever defining what success actually meant.

The realization shook him deeply.

A few weeks later, Adrian began working with a therapist specializing in high-performing entrepreneurs and post-liquidity transitions. Initially he resisted the process. Like many founders, he believed emotional struggle represented weakness.

But slowly, the conversations changed him.

He realized that the company had become his identity. Without constant survival pressure, he no longer knew who he was outside of work and achievement. Money had removed financial insecurity, but it had not automatically created purpose, peace, or fulfillment.

Over time, Adrian began rebuilding his life intentionally.

He stopped checking the stock price obsessively. He reduced public appearances and focused on authentic friendships. He created boundaries around financial requests from others. He began mentoring young founders privately rather than chasing media attention. He launched educational programs supporting students from low-income communities interested in artificial intelligence and engineering.

Most importantly, he slowed down enough to reconnect with himself emotionally.

One evening nearly three years after the IPO, Adrian sat quietly beside the ocean at his Malibu property watching the sunset. His phone buzzed repeatedly with financial alerts about market volatility.

For the first time in years, he ignored them.

Instead, he smiled softly to himself.

Because he finally understood something wealth alone could never teach him.

Success was not about becoming the richest person in the room.

It was about becoming someone who no longer needed external validation to feel complete.

Chapter 7

Creating Multi-Generational Wealth After an IPO

For many founders, executives, and early investors, going public represents the achievement of financial success beyond anything they once imagined possible. Years of sacrifice, uncertainty, and relentless work finally result in substantial liquidity and wealth creation. Yet one of the most important questions begins only after that wealth is created: Will the wealth survive beyond the current generation? Building wealth and preserving wealth are two entirely different challenges. Creating multi-generational wealth requires far more than investment returns alone. It demands vision, structure, discipline, education, governance, emotional intelligence, and long-term stewardship.

History repeatedly demonstrates that large fortunes often disappear surprisingly quickly. Many wealthy families lose substantial portions of their assets within two or three generations. The reasons are rarely purely financial. Wealth destruction typically occurs because of poor communication, lack of preparation, entitlement, emotional conflict, weak governance, excessive spending, fragmented leadership, or absence of shared purpose. Money itself is rarely the problem.

The real challenge is whether future generations develop the character, discipline, and financial understanding necessary to manage responsibility successfully.

Entrepreneurs who build companies capable of reaching the public markets often spend decades mastering business strategy, leadership, sales, operations, and risk-taking. However, few initially think deeply about family wealth governance during the startup phase. During those years, survival dominates attention. Yet after liquidity events occur, priorities often evolve. Founders begin asking larger questions about legacy, family stability, philanthropy, education, and long-term impact. Wealth preservation shifts from short-term accumulation toward creating durable systems designed to benefit future generations.

Multi-generational wealth begins with mindset. Many individuals mistakenly assume that leaving money alone is sufficient to create a legacy. In reality, financial capital without intellectual and emotional capital rarely survives. Future generations must understand not only how wealth was created, but also the values, discipline, sacrifice, and decision-making processes behind it. Without this foundation, inherited wealth can create complacency rather than empowerment. One of the most important principles of generational wealth is stewardship rather than ownership.

Stewardship means viewing wealth as something temporarily managed rather than permanently possessed. This mindset changes behavior dramatically. Instead of focusing solely on personal consumption or short-term gratification, stewards think in terms of continuity, responsibility, and long-term preservation. They ask how decisions made today will affect children, grandchildren, and future family stability decades later.

Family governance becomes increasingly important as wealth grows. Without clear governance structures, financial success can create conflict rather than unity. Disagreements over spending, investments, leadership roles, inheritance expectations, or business direction often intensify over time if systems are absent. Many wealthy families therefore establish formal governance frameworks designed to improve communication, define responsibilities, and maintain alignment across generations.

Family meetings are one example of effective governance. Sophisticated families often hold structured annual or quarterly meetings where investment strategies, charitable goals, educational initiatives, family values, and long-term planning are discussed openly. These meetings help younger generations gradually understand financial stewardship while strengthening communication and trust. Governance structures transform wealth management from isolated decision-making into collaborative long-term planning.

Education is perhaps the single most important component of preserving generational wealth. Financial literacy, investment knowledge, entrepreneurship, leadership skills, emotional intelligence, and personal discipline all matter significantly more than inheritance size alone. Families who successfully preserve wealth often prioritize education intensely, teaching children from an early age about money management, responsibility, delayed gratification, and long-term thinking.

Importantly, education should extend beyond technical financial concepts. Children must also understand the emotional and psychological realities of wealth. Without proper preparation, inherited wealth can create entitlement, dependency, lack of motivation, or emotional instability. Some wealthy families intentionally expose children to work, service, entrepreneurship, or financial responsibility early in life to build resilience and appreciation for effort.

Trust structures frequently play a major role in generational wealth planning. Trusts allow founders to establish rules governing how assets will be distributed, managed, and protected over time. Dynasty trusts, generation-skipping trusts, charitable trusts, and family limited partnerships can preserve assets while reducing estate taxes and protecting wealth from creditors, lawsuits, or poor financial decisions by future heirs.

However, trusts alone are not enough. Legal structures may protect assets mechanically, but they cannot create wisdom or emotional maturity automatically. Families who rely entirely on legal control without investing in communication and education often experience conflict despite sophisticated structures. Effective generational planning therefore combines technical legal strategy with intentional family development.

Philanthropy also becomes an important element of multi-generational wealth for many families. Shared charitable initiatives create opportunities for younger generations to understand purpose beyond financial accumulation alone. Family foundations, donor-advised funds, scholarship programs, healthcare initiatives, and community projects help align wealth with values and social contribution. Philanthropy can strengthen family identity while reducing the risk that future generations become consumed entirely by consumption or status.

Another major challenge in preserving generational wealth involves lifestyle inflation. As wealth expands, spending expectations often rise rapidly across generations. Expensive homes, luxury travel, private schools, social pressure, and elite lifestyles may become normalized. While there is nothing inherently wrong with enjoying wealth responsibly, unchecked lifestyle inflation can quietly erode even very large fortunes over time.

This risk becomes especially dangerous when younger generations inherit wealth without understanding cash flow, investment returns, taxes, or capital preservation. Spending habits disconnected from financial reality eventually become unsustainable. Families who preserve wealth successfully often maintain a culture of discipline and intentionality even after achieving extraordinary financial success.

Entrepreneurship itself can also become part of generational wealth strategy. Some founders intentionally encourage younger family members to build businesses, develop independent careers, or create value outside the family fortune. This approach reduces dependency while preserving ambition and personal identity. The goal is not merely to pass down money, but to pass down capability and confidence.

Family offices often support these efforts by coordinating investment management, tax planning, governance systems, educational programs, philanthropy, and succession planning. As discussed previously, family offices help organize complexity while maintaining long-term strategic continuity. For multi-generational families, these systems provide operational stability as wealth structures become increasingly sophisticated.

Succession planning also becomes critically important. Many founders struggle emotionally with delegation or leadership transition because their businesses represent personal identity. Yet failure to plan succession carefully can destabilize both family relationships and financial systems. Successful generational transitions require preparing future leaders gradually while creating clear expectations and governance processes.

Communication is another underestimated component of wealth preservation. Many families avoid discussing money openly because it feels uncomfortable emotionally. However, secrecy often creates confusion, mistrust, unrealistic expectations, or conflict later. Transparent communication about values, goals, responsibilities, and long-term vision significantly improves family stability over time.

Another important principle is adaptability. Economic conditions, tax laws, industries, technologies, and social norms evolve continuously across generations. Wealth preservation systems must therefore remain flexible enough to adapt without abandoning core principles. Families that become rigid or complacent often struggle during changing economic environments.

Psychological resilience matters enormously in generational planning as well. Market downturns, business failures, legal disputes, recessions, or personal crises are inevitable over long time horizons. Families who survive across generations usually develop emotional resilience alongside financial sophistication. They understand that wealth preservation requires patience, discipline, and perspective during difficult periods.

One of the greatest dangers to generational wealth is entitlement without responsibility. Children raised around significant wealth may struggle to develop motivation, gratitude, or work ethic if boundaries and expectations are unclear. Some wealthy parents unintentionally weaken future generations by removing all struggle from their lives. While financial support can create opportunities, excessive comfort may reduce resilience and personal growth.

For this reason, many successful founders emphasize values over wealth itself. Integrity, humility, discipline, curiosity, service, and accountability become central family principles. Wealth is treated as a tool supporting these values rather than replacing them. Long-term family success ultimately depends more on culture than capital alone. The emotional relationship future generations develop toward money also matters deeply. Some heirs become fearful about preserving wealth. Others become reckless because they never experienced financial hardship personally. Healthy stewardship requires balanced emotional understanding rather than anxiety or excess. Families that discuss money openly and thoughtfully often navigate these dynamics more effectively.

Importantly, multi-generational wealth does not necessarily mean creating permanent dynasties of passive heirs. The most successful wealth transitions often empower future generations to build meaningful lives independently while benefiting from family stability and opportunity. The objective is not merely preserving numbers on balance sheets, but creating environments where future generations can thrive responsibly.

The IPO may create the initial financial foundation, but generational wealth depends on what happens afterward. It depends on whether founders build systems strong enough to survive beyond their own leadership. It depends on whether values accompany assets. It depends on whether future generations receive preparation alongside inheritance.

Ultimately, multi-generational wealth is about far more than money itself. It is about continuity, opportunity, responsibility, and purpose. It is about creating stability without destroying ambition. It is about protecting freedom while encouraging growth. The greatest financial legacies are rarely measured solely by net worth. They are measured by whether future generations become capable, grounded, responsible, and empowered human beings.

The true success of post-IPO wealth is not determined by how much money exists during one founder's lifetime. It is determined by whether that wealth continues creating positive impact, stability, and opportunity long after the founder is gone.

The Family Meeting That Changed the Bennett Legacy Forever

Richard Bennett built his company the same way he approached almost everything in life—with relentless intensity.

When he founded Apex Infrastructure Solutions in his late twenties, he was driven almost entirely by survival. His father had worked construction jobs his entire life and died with very little savings. Richard grew up watching financial stress consume his family constantly. He promised himself early that his children would never experience the same instability.

For nearly twenty years, he worked obsessively.

He missed birthdays, vacations, anniversaries, and countless family dinners while building Apex into one of the largest engineering and infrastructure firms in the country. The sacrifices eventually paid off. When the company went public, Richard's ownership stake was suddenly worth nearly $780 million.

Financially, he had achieved everything he once dreamed about.

But privately, his family relationships were strained.

His wife, Laura, often felt disconnected from him emotionally. His oldest son, Tyler, drifted through life without direction despite attending elite schools. His daughter Sophia rarely discussed personal matters with him anymore. Richard told himself the sacrifices were temporary and necessary.

"We'll have time later," he always said.

Yet after the IPO, something unexpected happened.

Instead of bringing the family closer together, the wealth seemed to create even more distance.

Tyler began spending recklessly almost immediately. Luxury cars, expensive vacations, private clubs, and constant partying became normal. Sophia became increasingly anxious about money conversations altogether. Extended family members requested loans and investments constantly. Holiday gatherings became tense whenever financial topics surfaced.

One evening Richard sat alone in his massive home office reviewing investment reports when Laura walked in quietly.

“You built the financial empire,” she said softly. “But I’m not sure we built a family around it.”

Her words hit him harder than any business failure ever had.

Over the following months, Richard began reflecting deeply on his own childhood. His father had left very little financially, but he had passed down discipline, humility, work ethic, and resilience. Richard suddenly realized he had focused almost entirely on building assets while neglecting the systems and communication needed to preserve meaning around those assets.

The realization frightened him.

He had seen wealthy families collapse before. He knew stories of fortunes destroyed within one or two generations because children inherited money without preparation or purpose.

Richard decided things needed to change.

He contacted a family governance advisor named Caroline Hayes who specialized in helping wealthy entrepreneurial families navigate generational transitions.

During their first meeting, Caroline asked him a simple question.

“What values do you want your family wealth to represent?”

Richard paused silently.

No investment banker had ever asked him that.

For years he focused entirely on growth, valuation, and expansion. Yet now he realized something deeper mattered more.

“I want my children to have opportunities,” he finally said. “But I don’t want the money to destroy their ambition.”

Caroline nodded knowingly.

“That’s the real challenge,” she replied.

Over the next year, the Bennett family began holding structured quarterly family meetings for the first time.

Initially, the conversations felt awkward.

Tyler resisted openly.

"This feels like some corporate board meeting," he complained.

But gradually, the discussions changed the family dynamic.

Instead of avoiding money conversations, they began discussing values, long-term goals, philanthropy, responsibility, investing, and legacy openly. Richard explained the sacrifices and risks behind building Apex. Laura discussed the emotional cost of wealth without balance. Sophia became deeply interested in charitable projects supporting engineering education for low-income students.

Caroline also encouraged the family to establish clearer governance structures. Trusts and estate plans were updated. Financial education programs were introduced for younger family members. Spending expectations and investment responsibilities were discussed honestly instead of assumed silently.

Most importantly, Richard changed personally.

For the first time in decades, he prioritized relationships as intentionally as he once prioritized business growth.

One afternoon, Tyler visited Richard privately after a family meeting.

"I used to think the money was the important part," Tyler admitted quietly.

Richard looked at him carefully.

"What do you think now?"

Tyler hesitated. "I think you were trying to build security because you grew up without it."

Richard felt emotion rise unexpectedly in his chest.

For years, he assumed his children would never understand the deeper reasons behind his obsession with success.

But now, for the first time, real understanding was forming.

Over the following years, the Bennett family foundation funded scholarships, community infrastructure programs, and entrepreneurship education initiatives nationwide. Tyler eventually launched his own engineering startup instead of relying entirely on inherited wealth. Sophia led several philanthropic initiatives focused on financial literacy and education.

The family wealth continued growing steadily through disciplined governance and diversified investing.

But more importantly, the family itself became stronger.

Years later, during a retreat at the family ranch in Colorado, Richard sat beside Laura watching their grandchildren play outside beneath the mountains.

“You know what’s strange?” he said quietly.

“What?”

“I used to think leaving money behind was the goal.”

Laura smiled softly.

“And now?”

Richard watched his family laughing together in the distance.

“Now I realize the real legacy is what the money helps protect.”

Chapter 8

Philanthropy, Impact Investing, and Using Wealth for Purpose After an IPO

For many founders, executives, and early investors, the years leading up to an IPO are dominated by survival, ambition, competition, and growth. The company becomes the center of life. Every decision revolves around scaling operations, increasing revenue, attracting investors, building products, hiring talent, and outperforming competitors. During this phase, wealth creation often appears to be the ultimate destination. Yet after liquidity finally arrives and financial freedom becomes real, many wealthy individuals begin confronting a deeper question that money alone cannot answer: What is this wealth actually for?

This question represents one of the most important psychological and philosophical transitions after an IPO. Financial success creates options, flexibility, and security, but lasting fulfillment often requires something beyond accumulation itself. Many founders eventually realize that wealth without meaning can feel surprisingly empty. As a result, philanthropy, charitable initiatives, social impact projects, and purpose-driven investing increasingly become central parts of post-IPO life. Historically, some of the world's most influential entrepreneurs eventually shifted major portions of their attention toward philanthropy and impact. After achieving extraordinary financial success, they recognized that wealth could become a tool not only for personal freedom but also for creating positive change at scale. Education, healthcare, scientific research, environmental sustainability, poverty reduction, technological access, and community development all became areas where entrepreneurial wealth could influence society long after business success was achieved.

Philanthropy after an IPO is not simply about donating money. At its highest level, it becomes an intentional strategy for aligning wealth with values, purpose, and long-term impact. Sophisticated philanthropy involves vision, structure, measurement, leadership, and strategic thinking very similar to building a successful business. The goal is not merely charitable giving for appearances or tax deductions. The deeper goal is creating meaningful outcomes that improve lives and solve real-world problems.

One of the first realizations many wealthy founders experience is that money alone does not automatically create impact. Large donations without clear strategy may produce limited long-term results. Effective philanthropy requires understanding systems, incentives, leadership, accountability, and measurable outcomes. Some entrepreneurs bring the same disciplined thinking they used in business into their charitable initiatives, creating scalable organizations capable of generating significant social change.

Education often becomes one of the most popular areas of philanthropic focus for entrepreneurs. Many founders recognize how dramatically opportunity and knowledge influenced their own success. Scholarships, financial literacy programs, entrepreneurship training, technology education, and access initiatives can transform lives across generations. Founders who grew up in financially difficult environments often feel especially connected to creating opportunities for underserved communities.

Healthcare and medical research also attract significant post-IPO philanthropy. Entrepreneurs who witnessed illness, inadequate healthcare access, or medical challenges within their families frequently support hospitals, research institutions, disease prevention initiatives, and mental health programs. Technological founders, in particular, increasingly fund biotechnology research, AI-assisted healthcare solutions, and global health initiatives designed to scale impact through innovation.

Environmental sustainability has become another major focus for wealthy entrepreneurs after liquidity events. Climate change, renewable energy, conservation, clean water access, sustainable agriculture, and carbon reduction technologies increasingly attract philanthropic and investment capital. Many founders recognize that long-term wealth preservation itself depends on broader economic and environmental stability across future generations.

One important distinction wealthy individuals eventually learn is the difference between philanthropy and impact investing. Traditional philanthropy involves donating capital without expecting financial returns. Impact investing, however, seeks both financial returns and measurable social or environmental outcomes simultaneously. This model has become increasingly popular among entrepreneurs because it aligns business thinking with long-term societal goals.

Impact investments may include renewable energy projects, affordable housing developments, healthcare technology platforms, education systems, agricultural innovation, or financial inclusion initiatives. Investors seek opportunities where capital not only grows financially but also contributes positively to communities or global challenges. This approach allows wealthy individuals to align their investment portfolios with personal values while maintaining financial discipline.

The rise of environmental, social, and governance investing reflects this broader trend. Many investors increasingly evaluate companies not only by profitability but also by their environmental practices, labor policies, governance standards, and societal impact. Founders who spent years building companies often become more conscious of how capital allocation shapes the future of industries and communities.

Donor-advised funds have become one of the most widely used philanthropic structures after IPOs and liquidity events. These accounts allow individuals to contribute appreciated assets such as company stock, receive immediate tax deductions, and distribute charitable grants gradually over time. Donor-advised funds provide flexibility while improving tax efficiency, particularly when funded with highly appreciated public shares.

Private foundations represent another common philanthropic structure for ultra-high-net-worth individuals. Foundations allow families to build long-term charitable institutions capable of funding projects, hiring staff, creating educational programs, awarding grants, and involving future generations in philanthropy. Some families use foundations as tools for governance and values transmission across generations, helping children understand responsibility and stewardship.

However, philanthropy also introduces emotional and psychological complexity. Newly wealthy individuals often feel pressure to give publicly or solve large societal problems immediately after liquidity events. Friends, nonprofits, universities, and organizations may aggressively seek donations. Without clear priorities and boundaries, founders can become overwhelmed by constant requests and emotional expectations.

Some individuals also struggle with "philanthropic guilt," feeling morally obligated to solve every problem because of their financial capacity. Others donate impulsively without strategy, later realizing the giving lacked meaningful long-term impact. Effective philanthropy requires clarity, intentionality, and emotional discipline rather than reactive generosity alone.

Another challenge involves balancing personal wealth preservation with charitable ambitions. Some founders donate too aggressively early in their wealth journey before fully understanding long-term financial needs, taxes, family responsibilities, or market cycles. Others delay giving indefinitely while endlessly pursuing larger financial milestones. Sustainable philanthropy often requires balance between personal security and social contribution.

Entrepreneurs frequently bring unique strengths into philanthropy because they understand systems, scalability, leadership, and execution. Rather than simply writing checks, many founders actively participate in building organizations, improving operations, mentoring leadership teams, and developing innovative funding models. Their business experience often increases the effectiveness of charitable initiatives significantly.

Technology has also transformed modern philanthropy. Wealthy entrepreneurs increasingly use data analytics, AI systems, digital platforms, and measurable performance metrics to evaluate charitable outcomes. This "venture philanthropy" approach emphasizes accountability, measurable progress, scalability, and operational efficiency. While some critics argue philanthropy should not operate exactly like business, many entrepreneurs believe disciplined execution improves long-term impact substantially.

One of the most meaningful aspects of philanthropy after an IPO is the opportunity to reconnect wealth with human purpose. During the intense growth years leading to a public offering, founders often sacrifice personal balance, relationships, and emotional well-being while pursuing business goals. Charitable work sometimes helps restore perspective by reconnecting individuals with community, empathy, and broader societal contribution.

Philanthropy can also strengthen family relationships and generational continuity. Many wealthy families involve children and future heirs in charitable projects early, teaching values of service, gratitude, and stewardship. Shared philanthropic initiatives often create stronger emotional bonds than financial discussions alone. Giving becomes not only a financial act but also a cultural and educational tool within the family system.

Importantly, meaningful impact does not always require billion-dollar foundations or global initiatives. Some founders create enormous value through local community investments, mentorship programs, educational access initiatives, or direct support for entrepreneurs and families in need. The scale of wealth matters less than the intentionality and consistency behind its use.

Another powerful realization many wealthy individuals experience is that purpose-driven wealth often creates greater emotional fulfillment than consumption-driven wealth. Luxury lifestyles may provide temporary excitement, but meaningful contribution frequently produces deeper and more lasting satisfaction. Human beings naturally seek meaning, connection, and significance beyond personal accumulation alone.

This does not mean wealth itself is negative or that successful entrepreneurs should feel guilty about financial achievement. On the contrary, wealth creation through innovation, entrepreneurship, and value creation often benefits society enormously. However, after basic financial security and freedom are achieved, many individuals naturally seek broader forms of fulfillment that money alone cannot provide.

One of the greatest opportunities after an IPO is the ability to think beyond survival and begin shaping long-term societal impact intentionally. Financial freedom creates the capacity to support ideas, people, communities, and innovations that may otherwise struggle for resources. Wealth becomes a form of leverage capable of influencing future generations positively when deployed wisely.

Ultimately, philanthropy and impact investing represent more than financial activities. They represent a shift in perspective from accumulation toward contribution. They reflect the understanding that success is not measured solely by personal net worth, but also by the positive influence created through that wealth over time.

The IPO may create financial opportunity, but purpose

determines how that opportunity is ultimately used. Lasting fulfillment rarely comes from wealth alone. It comes from aligning resources with values, contribution, relationships, and long-term meaning. In the end, the greatest legacies are often not the fortunes people accumulate, but the lives they improve because of what they chose to do with that fortune.

The Scholarship Letter That Changed Victor Lang Forever

Victor Lang built his fortune by solving problems faster than everyone else.

As founder of NovaGrid Energy Systems, he spent fifteen years developing advanced renewable energy infrastructure software that transformed how utility companies managed electricity distribution. Investors admired his intensity. Employees respected his discipline. Competitors feared his relentless focus.

By the time NovaGrid went public, Victor's ownership stake exceeded $900 million.

The IPO made headlines across financial media. Analysts praised him as a visionary leader helping reshape the future of clean energy. Interviews, conferences, and investment opportunities flooded his schedule immediately after the public offering.

At first, Victor embraced the excitement.

He purchased a massive estate outside San Francisco, upgraded every aspect of his lifestyle, and expanded his investment portfolio aggressively. His calendar filled with elite networking events, private investor dinners, and high-profile business opportunities.

But privately, something felt strangely incomplete.

One evening after a major conference in New York, Victor sat alone in his hotel suite overlooking the city skyline. Financial news channels played quietly in the background discussing billionaire rankings and technology valuations.

He muted the television and stared silently out the window.

For years he believed reaching financial freedom would create permanent fulfillment. Yet despite the enormous success, he felt emotionally disconnected from his own life.

A few weeks later, while sorting through personal mail that had accumulated during months of travel, Victor noticed a handwritten envelope from a small community college in Arizona.

Curious, he opened it.

Inside was a letter from a nineteen-year-old engineering student named Elena Morales.

The letter explained that years earlier, NovaGrid had sponsored a small scholarship program for low-income students pursuing renewable energy studies. Elena described growing up in a struggling household where college seemed financially impossible. The scholarship allowed her to continue her education and eventually secure an internship at an energy technology company.

Near the end of the letter, one sentence stopped Victor completely.

"You probably don't realize it," she wrote, "but your company changed the direction of my entire life."

Victor sat frozen in silence.

For years he had focused almost entirely on valuations, growth metrics, market share, and shareholder returns. Yet this simple letter affected him more deeply than any IPO headline or financial milestone ever had.

The next day, Victor canceled several meetings and spent hours thinking alone.

For the first time in years, he asked himself a question unrelated to business growth:

"What do I actually want my wealth to accomplish?"

That question began changing everything.

Over the following months, Victor became increasingly interested in philanthropy and impact investing. Initially he approached it cautiously, worried about becoming emotionally reactive or inefficient. He studied philanthropic models, met with social impact investors, and spoke with nonprofit leaders and educators.

What surprised him most was how similar meaningful philanthropy felt to building a business.

The same principles mattered: leadership, scalability, accountability, execution, and long-term vision.

Victor eventually launched the Lang Future Energy Foundation focused on renewable energy education, engineering scholarships, and sustainable infrastructure development in underserved communities. But unlike traditional charity alone, he also began funding impact-driven startups developing affordable clean energy technologies for lower-income regions around the world.

The work changed him emotionally.

For the first time since the IPO, he felt deeply connected to something larger than personal wealth accumulation. He spent more time visiting schools, speaking with students, and mentoring young entrepreneurs than attending elite investor parties. One afternoon, while visiting a technical college funded through his foundation, Victor met Elena Morales in person for the first time.

She guided him through a student engineering lab filled with solar prototypes and renewable energy systems built by scholarship recipients.

"These students remind me of myself," Victor admitted quietly while walking through the classroom.

Elena smiled. "The difference is they now believe opportunities exist for them."

Her words stayed with him long after the visit ended.

Several years later, NovaGrid remained an enormously successful public company. Victor's wealth continued growing substantially through diversified investments and disciplined financial management.

But his life no longer revolved around net worth rankings or market fluctuations.

During an interview at a global sustainability conference, a journalist asked him a question.

“What has been the most rewarding part of becoming wealthy?”

Victor paused thoughtfully before answering. “For years,” he said quietly, “I thought success meant building a valuable company.”

He looked toward the audience of students and entrepreneurs seated throughout the conference hall.

“Now I think real success is using that value to help other people build meaningful futures too.”

Chapter 9

Preparing for Market Downturns and Protecting Wealth During Economic Cycles

One of the greatest mistakes newly wealthy founders, executives, and investors make after an IPO is assuming that strong markets will continue indefinitely. During periods of rapid growth and rising valuations, optimism becomes contagious. Stock prices climb, liquidity expands, investors become aggressive, and wealth appears to multiply effortlessly. In these environments, many individuals begin believing their success is permanent and that future appreciation will continue automatically. Yet financial history repeatedly demonstrates that economic cycles are inevitable. Bull markets eventually slow. Corrections occur. Recessions emerge. Liquidity tightens. Fear replaces optimism. The true test of long-term wealth preservation is not how individuals perform during easy markets, but how effectively they protect capital during difficult ones.

For founders transitioning from private entrepreneurship into public market wealth, this lesson becomes critically important. During the startup phase, risk-taking often produces extraordinary rewards. Aggressive growth strategies, concentrated exposure, leverage, and relentless optimism may all contribute to building a successful company. However, the same mindset that creates wealth can become dangerous after liquidity events if risk management is ignored. Once significant wealth exists, preservation becomes just as important as growth.

Economic cycles are not anomalies. They are natural components of financial systems. Markets move through periods of expansion and contraction influenced by interest rates, inflation, consumer confidence, corporate earnings, geopolitical events, technological shifts, and investor psychology. These cycles impact every asset class differently. Public equities, private investments, real estate, venture capital, commodities, and fixed income all respond uniquely to changing economic conditions. Understanding these relationships helps wealthy individuals build resilient financial systems capable of surviving uncertainty.

One of the most dangerous emotional states during strong markets is overconfidence. Rising valuations create the illusion that risk has disappeared. Investors become comfortable with leverage, concentrated positions, speculative assets, and aggressive spending because recent success reinforces confidence. However, prolonged bull markets often encourage behavior that becomes extremely painful during downturns. History repeatedly shows that the greatest financial damage usually occurs not during crises themselves, but during the periods of excessive optimism preceding them.

Technology bubbles, housing booms, speculative manias, and leverage-driven expansions all follow similar emotional patterns. During these phases, market participants convince themselves that "this time is different." Traditional valuation concerns are dismissed. Risk management appears unnecessary because prices continue rising. Wealthy individuals often expand lifestyles, increase debt, and take larger investment risks precisely when caution should be increasing.

For post-IPO shareholders, this risk becomes especially significant because much of their wealth may still remain tied to public equity markets. Founders who recently experienced dramatic stock appreciation often feel emotionally invincible during bull markets. Yet public markets are inherently volatile. A founder's net worth may decline by 30%, 50%, or more during severe downturns if diversification and liquidity planning were neglected.

Preparing for downturns therefore requires intentional humility. Wealth preservation begins with accepting that uncertainty is unavoidable. No founder, investor, economist, or institution can predict markets perfectly. The objective is not eliminating risk entirely, but building systems capable of surviving unexpected events without catastrophic damage.

Diversification remains one of the most important tools for protecting wealth during economic cycles. Concentrated exposure to one stock, sector, or asset class creates vulnerability because downturns rarely impact all investments equally. A diversified portfolio spreads risk across multiple categories including equities, bonds, real estate, cash reserves, international exposure, private investments, and income-producing assets. Diversification does not guarantee profits, but it significantly improves long-term resilience.

Liquidity is another essential component of downturn protection. Many wealthy individuals become overexposed to illiquid investments during strong markets. Private equity funds, venture capital investments, speculative startups, luxury real estate, and alternative assets may appear highly attractive during periods of optimism. However, illiquid assets become problematic during recessions because they cannot easily be converted into cash when opportunities or emergencies arise.

Cash reserves often appear boring during bull markets because they generate lower returns than aggressive investments. Yet during downturns, liquidity becomes extraordinarily valuable. Cash provides optionality. It allows investors to avoid forced selling during market declines while creating opportunities to acquire undervalued assets when others are panicking. Some of the greatest fortunes in history were expanded during recessions because disciplined investors maintained liquidity while competitors became financially trapped.

Debt management also plays a major role in wealth protection. Leverage amplifies both gains and losses. During rising markets, borrowing against assets may appear efficient and low-risk. However, leveraged positions become dangerous during downturns because falling asset values can trigger margin calls, forced liquidations, or refinancing problems. Many individuals who appear extremely wealthy during bull markets become financially distressed during recessions due to excessive leverage.

Founders after an IPO sometimes borrow aggressively against concentrated stock positions to fund luxury lifestyles, speculative investments, or real estate acquisitions. While this strategy may work temporarily during rising markets, it becomes extremely risky when stock prices decline sharply. Wealth preservation therefore often requires balancing growth ambitions with conservative financial structure. Fixed-income investments and defensive assets become increasingly important during volatile periods. Bonds, Treasury securities, dividend-producing assets, and certain types of infrastructure investments may provide stability when equities decline. While these assets may generate lower returns during bull markets, they help reduce overall portfolio volatility and preserve purchasing power during uncertain economic conditions.

Real estate behaves differently across economic cycles as well. Income-producing real estate with strong cash flow and conservative financing may provide stability during inflationary environments or equity market volatility. However, speculative real estate purchased with excessive leverage can become highly vulnerable during recessions. Understanding the difference between stable cash-flowing assets and speculative appreciation-driven investments is critical.

Another major challenge during downturns is emotional discipline. Fear becomes contagious during economic crises. Negative headlines dominate media coverage. Market volatility increases dramatically. Investors panic and often sell quality assets at precisely the wrong time. Emotional reactions destroy more wealth during recessions than the downturns themselves.

The ability to remain rational during periods of uncertainty becomes one of the defining characteristics of successful long-term wealth management. Investors who built disciplined systems before downturns are far more likely to make thoughtful decisions during crises. Those operating emotionally often swing between greed during bull markets and panic during recessions, creating destructive cycles of poor timing.

Historical perspective helps strengthen emotional resilience. Financial crises, while painful, are recurring parts of economic history. Markets have survived wars, recessions, inflationary periods, banking collapses, political instability, and technological disruptions repeatedly over decades. Long-term wealth preservation therefore depends less on avoiding every downturn and more on surviving them without permanent impairment.

One important principle many wealthy families follow is stress testing. Rather than assuming optimistic conditions, they evaluate how portfolios and lifestyles would perform under severe economic stress. What happens if equities fall 40%? What happens if real estate declines significantly? What happens if liquidity disappears temporarily? Stress testing exposes vulnerabilities before crises occur.

Insurance and legal asset protection strategies also contribute to downturn resilience. Liability exposure, lawsuits, business risks, cybersecurity threats, and unexpected crises may increase during economic instability. Wealth preservation therefore requires protecting not only investment portfolios but also broader financial structures surrounding those assets.

Entrepreneurs often possess natural optimism and high risk tolerance because these traits helped them build successful companies initially. However, long-term wealth stewardship requires balancing optimism with realism. Economic cycles are not personal failures. They are structural realities of markets and capitalism itself. Accepting this reality encourages preparation rather than complacency.

Family communication becomes particularly important during downturns as well. Wealthy families who openly discuss financial planning, spending discipline, and long-term perspective tend to navigate crises more effectively than families avoiding difficult conversations. Panic decreases when systems and expectations are clearly understood.

One of the greatest advantages wealthy individuals possess during recessions is the ability to think long term. Those with sufficient liquidity, low leverage, and disciplined planning can often acquire extraordinary opportunities during downturns when fear dominates markets. Recessions frequently create discounted valuations across businesses, real estate, equities, and private investments. Investors prepared psychologically and financially for these moments often emerge significantly stronger afterward.

Importantly, preparing for downturns does not mean living in constant fear or avoiding growth entirely. The objective is balance. Wealth should continue compounding productively while remaining protected against catastrophic loss. Sustainable wealth preservation requires participating in growth opportunities without becoming emotionally or financially dependent on permanently rising markets.

Another valuable lesson during economic cycles is recognizing the difference between temporary volatility and permanent destruction. Market declines themselves are normal. The real danger arises when poor decisions during downturns permanently impair capital or destroy financial flexibility. Forced selling, excessive leverage, panic liquidation, or unsustainable lifestyle obligations often create lasting damage far beyond the downturn itself.

The most successful long-term investors and founders understand that survival matters more than perfection. No one consistently predicts market timing accurately. Yet disciplined preparation dramatically improves resilience. Wealth that survives recessions retains the ability to recover, compound, and grow during future expansions. Ultimately, preparing for downturns is not pessimism—it is maturity. It reflects an understanding that markets move through cycles and that financial security depends on preparation rather than optimism alone. The IPO may create wealth during favorable market conditions, but preserving that wealth across decades requires surviving the inevitable periods when conditions become difficult.

True financial freedom is not measured by how wealthy someone appears during bull markets. It is measured by how stable, flexible, and emotionally grounded they remain when markets become uncertain. The individuals who build lasting wealth are rarely those who avoid all downturns. They are the ones who prepare intelligently, remain disciplined, and emerge from difficult cycles stronger than before.

The Crash That Taught Julian Mercer the Meaning of Real Wealth

Julian Mercer loved bull markets.

As founder of TitanFlow Robotics, he had spent nearly fifteen years building one of the most advanced industrial automation companies in the world. The IPO transformed him overnight from a respected entrepreneur into one of the wealthiest founders in the technology sector.

At the peak of the market frenzy, Julian's net worth surpassed $2.4 billion.

Financial media praised his aggressive leadership style constantly. Investors admired his confidence. Young entrepreneurs viewed him as proof that fearless risk-taking created extraordinary success.

And Julian believed it completely.

The years immediately following the IPO felt unstoppable.

TitanFlow's stock climbed relentlessly as investors poured money into artificial intelligence and automation companies. Julian expanded his lifestyle aggressively. He purchased a 20,000-square-foot estate in Beverly Hills, multiple vacation homes, a yacht, and several private aviation memberships. He invested heavily into speculative startups and crypto-related ventures recommended by wealthy friends.

But perhaps most dangerously, he borrowed aggressively against his TitanFlow shares.

Private banks eagerly extended enormous credit lines because his stock holdings appeared incredibly valuable and stable. Julian viewed leverage as sophisticated financial strategy.

"Why sell appreciating assets," he often told advisors, "when you can borrow cheaply against them?"

At first, the strategy appeared brilliant.

His investments soared alongside the broader market. Every month his net worth increased further. Financial magazines ranked him among the top-performing tech founders in the country.

Then everything changed.

Inflation surged unexpectedly across the economy. Interest rates rose rapidly. Investor sentiment shifted almost overnight. High-growth technology stocks began collapsing.

TitanFlow initially resisted the decline.

Then several major manufacturing clients delayed expansion projects due to economic uncertainty. Quarterly growth slowed. Analysts downgraded the stock aggressively.

Within six months, TitanFlow's shares fell nearly 45%.

Julian remained publicly confident.

"This is temporary volatility," he insisted during interviews.

But privately, panic began creeping into his life.

Because so much of his lifestyle and investment structure depended on leverage tied to TitanFlow stock, the falling share price created mounting pressure. Banks requested additional collateral. Some speculative investments became nearly worthless. Real estate markets softened simultaneously.

Then came the margin calls.

One afternoon Julian sat silently inside his home office staring at a series of urgent financial notices spread across his desk.

For the first time since the IPO, he realized something terrifying.

Most of his wealth had been built on assumptions that markets would continue rising indefinitely.

That evening his longtime advisor, Rebecca Sloan, arrived for an emergency meeting.

She reviewed the numbers carefully before speaking.

"You expanded your lifestyle around temporary valuations," she said calmly.

Julian rubbed his forehead exhausted. "I thought the growth would continue."

"Everyone thinks that during bull markets."

The next several months became the most painful financial period of Julian's life. He was forced to liquidate several properties. Many speculative investments collapsed completely. Media headlines that once praised him now criticized his aggressive leverage and spending habits. Friends who constantly surrounded him during prosperous years disappeared quietly.

For a while, Julian felt humiliated.

But the crisis slowly began changing him psychologically.

During long nights reviewing financial statements and restructuring obligations, he realized he had confused wealth with visibility, consumption, and rising valuations. He had optimized for appearing rich rather than building durable financial security.

That realization transformed his thinking completely.

Over the following years, Julian rebuilt his financial life with radically different principles.

He reduced leverage dramatically. He diversified systematically into income-producing assets, fixed income, infrastructure investments, and conservatively financed real estate. He maintained large liquidity reserves instead of maximizing speculative returns. Most importantly, he stopped emotionally tying his identity to market cycles.

The process felt less glamorous publicly.

But internally, he felt calmer than he had in years.

Several years later, another market downturn hit the economy unexpectedly. Financial media once again became consumed by fear and panic.

This time, however, Julian reacted differently.

While others rushed to liquidate assets emotionally, he quietly deployed cash reserves into discounted investments and distressed opportunities created by the recession. Because his financial structure was stable, the downturn became an opportunity rather than a threat.

One evening during the crisis, a young founder called Julian nervously seeking advice.

"I feel like everything is collapsing," the founder admitted. "How do you survive this?"

Julian looked out the window of his office thoughtfully before answering.

"You stop measuring wealth by how high you can fly during good times," he said quietly. "And you start measuring it by how stable you remain when everything gets difficult."

Chapter 10

The Ultimate Transition: From Founder to Long-Term Capital Allocator

For most entrepreneurs, the years leading up to an IPO are defined by obsession, intensity, and relentless execution. Founders spend enormous amounts of time solving operational problems, raising capital, hiring teams, managing crises, competing against rivals, and trying to survive long enough to reach scale. The company becomes their identity. Every day revolves around growth, momentum, and immediate decision-making. Yet after a successful IPO and significant liquidity event, another transition begins—one that is often far more difficult than building the company itself. The founder must evolve from entrepreneur into long-term capital allocator.

This transition represents one of the most important psychological, financial, and strategic shifts after going public. During the startup phase, wealth is typically created through concentrated effort in a single business. After liquidity, however, wealth preservation and expansion increasingly depend on how capital is allocated across multiple opportunities, economic cycles, industries, and generations. The founder who once managed employees, products, and investors now faces a much larger challenge: managing capital itself responsibly over decades.

Many founders underestimate how difficult this transition can be. Entrepreneurship rewards speed, optimism, risk-taking, and intense focus. Capital allocation, however, often rewards patience, discipline, emotional control, and long-term thinking. The traits that create startup success do not always translate automatically into effective wealth stewardship. Some founders continue operating as if every decision requires aggressive risk-taking, while others become paralyzed by fear after achieving financial success. The healthiest long-term outcomes usually come from balancing entrepreneurial ambition with disciplined financial structure.

At its core, capital allocation is the process of deciding where financial resources should be deployed to generate long-term value. Public markets, private businesses, venture investments, real estate, fixed income, philanthropy, infrastructure, technology, international opportunities, and family wealth systems all compete for attention and capital after an IPO. The founder's challenge becomes evaluating risk, opportunity, timing, liquidity, and purpose simultaneously.

One of the first realizations many founders experience after liquidity events is that having wealth and managing wealth are entirely different skills. Building a company may require vision, leadership, product innovation, and relentless determination. Managing substantial wealth requires understanding economics, taxation, portfolio construction, legal structures, market psychology, risk management, and long-term planning. The founder who refuses to evolve intellectually after an IPO often becomes vulnerable to poor financial decisions despite extraordinary business success.

Many wealthy entrepreneurs initially believe they can outperform in every investment category simply because they succeeded in business. This overconfidence can become dangerous. Financial history contains countless examples of successful founders who lost significant wealth through speculative investments, excessive leverage, emotional trading, or overestimating their expertise outside their core industry. Capital allocation requires humility because markets punish arrogance eventually.

The most effective capital allocators understand the importance of asymmetrical thinking. They seek opportunities where potential upside significantly outweighs downside risk. Rather than chasing excitement or trends emotionally, they evaluate probabilities carefully. They focus on preserving flexibility while allowing capital to compound over long periods of time. Long-term wealth creation often depends more on avoiding catastrophic losses than on achieving extraordinary short-term gains.

Compounding becomes one of the most important concepts after an IPO. Entrepreneurs often think in terms of rapid growth because startups operate in fast-moving environments. Yet long-term wealth preservation frequently relies on patient compounding over decades rather than explosive short-term returns alone. Small advantages sustained consistently over long periods produce extraordinary outcomes through the mathematics of compounded capital.

This principle applies not only to investments but also to relationships, reputation, knowledge, and systems. Founders who continue learning, building strong networks, protecting credibility, and improving decision-making frameworks compound intellectual and social capital alongside financial capital. The most powerful wealth ecosystems are rarely built through isolated decisions alone. They emerge through decades of disciplined accumulation across multiple dimensions.

Another critical lesson in capital allocation is understanding opportunity cost. Every investment decision involves tradeoffs. Deploying capital into one asset means that same capital cannot be used elsewhere. Wealthy individuals therefore learn to evaluate not merely potential returns, but also liquidity, flexibility, tax consequences, emotional stress, and long-term alignment with broader goals.

For example, some founders become excessively illiquid after IPOs by placing too much wealth into private equity, venture capital, speculative startups, or highly leveraged real estate. While these investments may offer high potential returns, they can reduce financial flexibility during economic downturns. Others become overly conservative out of fear, leaving large portions of capital stagnant and unproductive for years. Effective capital allocation balances growth opportunities with resilience and adaptability.

Public market investing often becomes one of the largest areas of adjustment for founders after an IPO. Entrepreneurs accustomed to controlling businesses directly may initially struggle with passive ownership structures. Unlike operating companies, public markets involve accepting uncertainty and allowing management teams, macroeconomic conditions, and market sentiment to influence outcomes. Some founders become frustrated by the lack of direct control and overtrade emotionally as a result.

The best long-term investors, however, recognize that disciplined portfolio construction and patience often outperform reactive behavior. They understand that volatility is normal and that emotional consistency matters more than perfect market timing. Many successful founders eventually adopt investment philosophies centered around quality businesses, durable cash flow, strong management, and long-term secular trends rather than speculative short-term trading.

Private investing and venture capital frequently remain attractive areas for entrepreneurs because these environments feel more familiar psychologically. Founders often enjoy mentoring younger entrepreneurs and participating in innovation ecosystems. However, venture investing also introduces emotional bias because founders may identify too strongly with startup culture and underestimate risk. Disciplined capital allocation requires separating emotional excitement from objective probability assessment.

Real estate often becomes another major allocation category after liquidity events. Income-producing real estate can provide stable cash flow, inflation protection, tax advantages, and diversification outside public equities. Yet real estate also carries operational complexity, leverage risk, geographic concentration, and cyclical exposure. Sophisticated investors evaluate real estate based on long-term fundamentals rather than emotional status symbolism.

International diversification becomes increasingly important as wealth expands as well. Many founders initially concentrate assets heavily within their domestic economy or industry because those environments feel familiar. However, global diversification reduces dependence on one country, currency, regulatory system, or economic cycle. International opportunities may also provide exposure to demographic growth, technological expansion, or resource development unavailable domestically.

Another essential aspect of capital allocation involves aligning investments with personal values and life goals. Wealth should not exist in isolation from purpose. Some founders prioritize maximizing financial returns indefinitely even after achieving enormous wealth, while others begin focusing more on family, philanthropy, social impact, or quality of life. There is no universally correct answer. However, sustainable fulfillment usually requires capital allocation decisions that align with deeper personal priorities rather than endless accumulation alone.

Time allocation becomes equally important after an IPO. Many founders assume wealth automatically creates freedom, yet they continue operating with the same chaotic schedules and emotional stress patterns developed during startup years. The healthiest long-term transitions often involve becoming intentional not only about money but also about time, relationships, health, learning, and personal growth.

Health itself becomes a critical but often overlooked form of capital. Entrepreneurs frequently sacrifice sleep, exercise, recovery, relationships, and emotional balance while building companies. After achieving financial success, some founders realize too late that wealth cannot fully compensate for neglected physical and mental health. Sustainable long-term freedom requires protecting personal well-being as carefully as financial assets.

Reputation also compounds over time. Founders who allocate capital ethically, communicate honestly, support meaningful causes, and treat people well often build networks and opportunities that extend far beyond financial returns alone. Conversely, arrogance, greed, or short-term opportunism can damage reputational capital permanently despite financial success. Long-term wealth preservation depends partly on maintaining trust and credibility across decades.

One of the most important mindset shifts after an IPO is recognizing that wealth management is not a sprint. The startup phase may reward urgency and constant intensity, but preserving and growing wealth across generations requires patience and emotional endurance. Economic cycles will continue. Markets will fluctuate. Opportunities will emerge and disappear repeatedly. Sustainable success depends less on reacting emotionally to every event and more on maintaining consistent principles over time.

Many founders eventually discover that the ultimate purpose of capital allocation is freedom. Freedom to choose projects intentionally. Freedom to support family and future generations. Freedom to contribute meaningfully to society. Freedom to pursue health, relationships, creativity, philanthropy, and purpose without constant financial anxiety. Money itself becomes less important than the flexibility and opportunity it provides.

The most successful long-term capital allocators therefore think differently from those trapped in short-term status competition. They optimize for durability rather than appearances. They value resilience over excitement. They prioritize optionality over ego. They focus on preserving the ability to continue making meaningful choices decades into the future.

Ultimately, the founder who evolves successfully after an IPO learns that true wealth is not measured solely by net worth. It is measured by how effectively capital supports a meaningful, stable, purposeful, and adaptable life. The IPO may create the initial financial foundation, but long-term capital allocation determines whether that foundation becomes temporary success or enduring freedom. The transition from entrepreneur to capital allocator is therefore not merely financial. It is philosophical. It requires redefining success beyond company valuation alone and recognizing that the highest form of wealth may ultimately be the ability to live intentionally, contribute meaningfully, and remain emotionally grounded regardless of market conditions.

The Day Cameron Blake Stopped Chasing Bigger Numbers

Cameron Blake built companies the same way some people fight wars.

Aggressively. Relentlessly. Obsessively.

From the time he launched his first logistics software startup in a rented warehouse at age twenty-six, his entire life revolved around winning. Investors admired his intensity. Employees feared disappointing him. Competitors struggled to keep pace with his ambition.

For nearly eighteen years, Cameron pushed forward nonstop.

He slept four or five hours a night. He missed family vacations. He skipped weddings, birthdays, and holidays. He measured success almost entirely through growth charts, revenue targets, acquisitions, and valuation increases. Eventually, it worked. His company, Quantis Global Systems, became one of the fastest-growing enterprise logistics platforms in the world. When the company went public, Cameron's ownership stake exceeded $1.8 billion.

The IPO launch felt surreal.

Financial media praised him constantly. Business magazines featured him on covers beside headlines calling him "The Architect of the Next Industrial Revolution." Venture firms competed for his attention. Conferences paid enormous speaking fees for appearances.

For a while, Cameron loved the attention.

But something strange happened after the IPO.

Instead of feeling complete, he felt restless.

No matter how high his net worth climbed, it never felt like enough. Every success quickly became normal. If his portfolio gained $100 million, he immediately focused on how it could gain another $500 million. He compared himself constantly against founders richer than he was. Billionaires became his new benchmark.

The chase never stopped.

At the same time, his personal life quietly deteriorated. His marriage became increasingly distant. His teenage son barely spoke to him during family dinners. Cameron's health worsened from years of stress, poor sleep, and nonstop travel. Yet he ignored all of it because the market rewarded his intensity financially.

Then came the recession.

A major global slowdown hit the technology and logistics sectors hard. Quantis stock fell sharply alongside the broader market. Cameron's paper wealth declined by nearly $700 million within one year.

The financial loss disturbed him emotionally far more than he expected.

For months he became obsessed with recovering the decline. He worked even harder, monitored markets constantly, and poured money aggressively into speculative opportunities hoping to accelerate gains again.

One evening after another exhausting day of meetings, Cameron returned to his penthouse overlooking Chicago. His son Ethan was sitting alone in the kitchen finishing homework.

Without looking up, Ethan asked quietly:

"Dad, when will enough actually be enough for you?"

The question hit Cameron harder than any market crash ever had. For the first time in years, he had no immediate answer.

That night he barely slept.

He walked through the empty apartment staring at the skyline while replaying the question repeatedly in his head. He realized he had spent decades optimizing for valuation instead of life itself.

The next morning, Cameron canceled several major meetings unexpectedly and flew alone to a small ranch property he owned in Montana but rarely visited.

For nearly a week, he disconnected almost entirely from financial media, investor calls, and market updates.

And slowly, clarity began returning.

He realized he had treated capital allocation like a competition rather than a tool. Every investment decision focused on maximizing numbers instead of maximizing freedom, meaning, or balance. Wealth had become a scoreboard instead of a foundation for a better life.

When Cameron returned, he began restructuring everything.

He diversified aggressively into stable income-producing assets instead of chasing only speculative growth. He reduced unnecessary leverage. He delegated more operational responsibilities. He spent more time with family. He invested in healthcare innovation, educational programs, and environmental infrastructure projects that aligned with personal values rather than pure hype cycles.

Most importantly, he changed emotionally.

For the first time since becoming wealthy, he stopped measuring his self-worth entirely through financial rankings.

Several years later, Cameron spoke privately with a younger founder preparing for an IPO.

The founder looked excited and nervous at the same time.

"What's the biggest mistake wealthy founders make after going public?" he asked.

Cameron smiled thoughtfully before answering.

"We spend years learning how to build companies," he said quietly. "But almost no one teaches us how to build a life after the company succeeds."

Final IPO Thoughts

Building Lasting Wealth Beyond the Public Markets

Going public is one of the most transformative financial events an entrepreneur, founder, executive, or early investor can experience. For many people, the IPO represents the realization of years of sacrifice, uncertainty, risk, stress, and relentless persistence. It symbolizes validation from investors, markets, media, and society. The company that once existed only as an idea, a vision, or a risky startup suddenly becomes a publicly traded organization recognized around the world. Wealth appears rapidly. Visibility expands dramatically. Opportunities multiply. Yet as this book has explored repeatedly, the IPO itself is not the final destination. It is the beginning of an entirely new phase of financial and personal responsibility.

Many individuals spend decades learning how to build wealth but very little time learning how to preserve it. Entrepreneurship rewards concentration, optimism, speed, and aggressive risk-taking. Those traits often help founders survive difficult startup years and eventually achieve extraordinary success. However, the same mindset that creates wealth may become dangerous after liquidity events if not balanced with discipline, planning, emotional maturity, and long-term thinking. The transition from entrepreneur to wealth steward is one of the most important shifts that occurs after a company enters the public markets.

One of the central lessons throughout this book is that paper wealth and real financial freedom are not the same thing. Public market valuations may fluctuate dramatically. Net worth may rise and fall by millions of dollars within days or even hours. Headlines may celebrate temporary success during bull markets while ignoring the deeper financial realities underneath. True wealth is not simply a number attached to a stock price. Real wealth is flexibility, security, liquidity, resilience, and peace of mind. It is the ability to maintain freedom and stability regardless of market volatility or economic cycles.

The founders and executives who preserve wealth successfully are usually not the individuals who chase the highest valuation at all costs. They are the ones who build systems capable of surviving uncertainty. They diversify intelligently. They prepare for taxes carefully. They maintain liquidity reserves. They reduce excessive leverage. They think long term. Most importantly, they separate emotional identity from temporary market conditions.

Public markets are powerful wealth creation engines, but they are also emotionally intense environments. Stock prices move constantly. Investor sentiment shifts rapidly. Economic cycles change unexpectedly. During bull markets, confidence often becomes excessive. During downturns, fear becomes overwhelming. Wealthy individuals who tie emotional stability entirely to market performance eventually experience exhaustion, anxiety, or destructive decision-making. Emotional discipline therefore becomes one of the most important forms of wealth protection after an IPO.

Another major lesson explored throughout this book is the importance of diversification. Many founders emotionally resist selling shares because their companies represent years of sacrifice, identity, and belief. Yet concentration risk remains one of the greatest threats to long-term financial stability. Even extraordinary companies face uncertainty over time. Industries evolve, technologies change, competition intensifies, and economic cycles fluctuate. Diversification is not a lack of confidence. It is recognition that uncertainty exists in every market and every business.

Tax strategy also plays a critical role in determining whether wealth survives across decades and generations. Taxes influence liquidity planning, diversification timing, estate structures, charitable giving, investment allocation, and family wealth transfer. Sophisticated planning before major liquidity events often creates enormous long-term advantages. Wealth preservation is not simply about maximizing returns. It is also about minimizing unnecessary financial erosion through inefficient structures and reactive decision-making.

As wealth grows, complexity increases. Family offices, trusts, governance systems, insurance strategies, philanthropic structures, and estate planning all become increasingly important. Without organization and coordination, even substantial fortunes can become fragmented, inefficient, or vulnerable to future conflict. The most successful families understand that preserving wealth requires systems, communication, education, and stewardship—not merely investment performance alone.

One of the deepest themes throughout this book has been the psychological transformation that follows sudden wealth creation. Going public changes far more than bank accounts. It changes identity, relationships, emotional patterns, and personal expectations. Many founders spend years believing financial success will finally create peace, happiness, or fulfillment, only to discover that wealth amplifies existing emotional realities rather than replacing them. Money removes certain stresses, but it does not automatically create meaning, purpose, or emotional balance. This realization often leads wealthy individuals toward philanthropy, impact investing, mentorship, family development, or broader societal contribution. Once survival and financial security are achieved, many people naturally begin asking deeper questions about legacy and purpose. What impact should this wealth create? What values should it support? How can financial success improve the lives of others beyond personal consumption alone?

The most meaningful legacies are rarely defined solely by valuation figures or net worth rankings. They are defined by the opportunities created, families strengthened, communities improved, and future generations empowered because of the wealth that was built. Financial success becomes most powerful when aligned with purpose, responsibility, and contribution.

Another critical lesson is understanding the inevitability of economic cycles. Markets do not move upward forever. Recessions, corrections, crises, inflationary periods, and market dislocations are recurring realities throughout financial history. Wealth that survives across generations is usually built by individuals who prepare for difficult periods before they arrive. Liquidity, conservative leverage, diversified assets, emotional discipline, and long-term perspective all become enormously valuable during downturns.

Many individuals appear wealthy during bull markets. Far fewer remain financially stable during periods of economic stress. The difference often comes down to preparation rather than intelligence alone. Sustainable wealth is not about avoiding every downturn. It is about ensuring that downturns do not permanently destroy financial flexibility or emotional stability.

One of the most powerful ideas in post-IPO wealth management is understanding the difference between temporary success and durable freedom. Temporary success may depend heavily on current valuations, market sentiment, or concentrated exposure. Durable freedom, however, exists when wealth becomes diversified, protected, liquid, and aligned with long-term personal goals. Durable freedom means the ability to live intentionally without constant fear of market collapse, financial instability, or identity loss tied to stock performance.

For many entrepreneurs, this transition requires redefining success itself. During the startup phase, success may mean survival, growth, valuation increases, or achieving liquidity. After an IPO, however, success often becomes more personal and nuanced. It may involve family stability, health, purpose, philanthropy, emotional peace, meaningful work, or generational continuity. The founder who learns to evolve beyond purely financial achievement often experiences far greater long-term fulfillment than the one endlessly chasing larger numbers alone.

This book has also emphasized the importance of humility. Markets are unpredictable. Economic conditions change. No founder, investor, or advisor possesses perfect foresight. Overconfidence destroys enormous amounts of wealth every market cycle. Humility encourages preparation, diversification, discipline, and openness to long-term planning. It allows wealthy individuals to recognize that preserving freedom matters more than proving invincibility.

At the same time, wealth should not be approached from a place of fear alone. The objective is not merely protecting assets endlessly while avoiding all opportunity. The objective is balance. Wealth exists to create options, flexibility, contribution, experiences, innovation, and meaningful impact. Intelligent wealth management allows individuals to participate confidently in future opportunities without risking total financial collapse.

The public markets provide extraordinary opportunities for wealth creation unlike anything previous generations experienced historically. Technology, globalization, entrepreneurship, and capital markets have allowed founders to create enormous value at unprecedented speed. Yet with this opportunity comes responsibility. Financial success without stewardship often disappears quickly. Wealth without purpose may feel empty. Liquidity without discipline becomes dangerous.

Ultimately, the most important realization after an IPO may be this: wealth is not the finish line. It is a tool. Like any tool, its long-term value depends entirely on how wisely it is used. Wealth can create freedom or pressure. It can strengthen families or divide them. It can support meaningful impact or fuel endless consumption. It can build long-term stability or disappear through emotional decision-making and poor planning.

The entrepreneurs who navigate post-IPO life most successfully are usually those who understand that financial freedom is not simply about having money. It is about creating a life where money supports deeper values rather than replacing them. It is about building systems that survive uncertainty. It is about maintaining emotional balance during success and adversity alike. It is about using wealth intentionally rather than reactively.

The IPO may place someone on the global financial stage, but what happens afterward ultimately defines the true legacy.

Some individuals become trapped chasing temporary valuations forever. Others evolve into thoughtful stewards of capital, family leaders, philanthropists, investors, mentors, and builders of long-term opportunity. The difference lies not in the size of the IPO itself, but in the mindset developed afterward.

As you move forward from this book, remember that long-term wealth preservation is not one decision. It is a lifelong process of adaptation, discipline, learning, and intentionality. Markets will rise and fall. Opportunities will appear and disappear. Economic conditions will change repeatedly. But individuals who remain grounded, prepared, diversified, emotionally disciplined, and purpose-driven are far more likely to transform temporary financial success into lasting freedom and enduring legacy.

The IPO may create wealth in a moment.

But wisdom determines whether that wealth lasts for generations.

www.ingramcontent.com/pod-product-compliance
Ingram Content Group UK Ltd.
Pitfield, Milton Keynes, MK11 3LW, UK
UKHW010011031026
15589UKWH00008B/1601

9 798256 015824